To my 'People' with extra special love from Trilly.
Xmas '82.

THE CREATIVE GIFT

THE CREATIVE GIFT

THE ARTS AND THE CHRISTIAN LIFE

H.R.ROOKMAAKER

Inter-Varsity Press

Inter-Varsity Press
38 De Montfort Street, Leicester LE1 7GP, England

First British edition 1982

Rookmaaker, H.R.
The creative gift: The arts and the Christian life
1. Christian life
I. Title
248.4 BV4501.2

ISBN 0-85110-706-0

Printed and bound in Great Britain by
Weatherby Woolnough, Wellingborough, Northants.

Set in 11/12½ pt Palatino.

Inter-Varsity Press is the publishing division of the Universities and Colleges Christian Fellowship (formerly the Inter-Varsity Fellowship), a student movement linking Christian Unions in universities and colleges throughout the British Isles, and a member movement of the International Fellowship of Evangelical Students. For information about local and national activities in Great Britain write to UCCF, 38 De Montfort Street, Leicester LE1 7GP.

CONTENTS

Grateful acknowledgement is made for permission to reprint the following copyright material:

'Letter to a Christian Artist,' from the September 2, 1966 issue of *Christianity Today* © 1966. Used by permission of *Christianity Today*.

'Howl' by Allen Ginsberg from *Howl and Other Poems,* Copyright © 1956, 1959 by Allen Ginsberg. Reprinted by permission of CITY LIGHT Books.

INTRODUCTION:
The Centre of History

We live in a wonderful world—a world that discloses itself to us through our senses, but is at the same time far more than what our senses alone can reveal. We see something moving, we recognize certain shapes, and we know that a human being is standing before us. Yet the merest glance tells us far more. By his clothing, his actions, or his expression we can tell what sort of man he is. So when we talk about "seeing," we mean much more than visual perception. We can "see" love or hatred, the beauty of a landscape, or the nobility of a sacrificial act. We can know someone has great faith, even though we cannot perceive it with our eyes. Although these things do not, scientifically speaking, belong to the senses, they are part of our daily experience; reality comprises much more than our senses alone can apprehend.

Even if we use all our human faculties, and add to the senses our experience and our knowledge, these can show us only a small part of the things that exist, for reality goes deeper than our familiar world. Many things in the world we see point to this other world. As the psalmist said when speaking of the forces of nature: "There is no speech or language where their voice is not heard. Their voice goes out into all the earth, their words to the ends of the world"

(Psalm 19:3, 4). Within this world is evidence of the other side (Romans 1:20), including the realms of Heaven where God dwells, and his angels and a whole order of reality. Yet God is not confined to the other side, for he is also the Creator and Lawgiver of the world as we know it, including everything we call secular, and even our own selves.

This same God has revealed himself to us, telling us who he is and what he expects of us. Through the men who wrote the Bible God has given us a glimpse of what is behind our empirical reality. He has provided us with insight into our world, its principles and structures. Because of this revelation, we have knowledge beyond the mere reach of our human faculties, but also more than we should have had even if man had never fallen into sin. We know, for example, that the world is not a closed system, but open; that it does not exist on its own; and that its center is not on the side of reality visible to man.

God gave such a glimpse as part of his revelation to St. John. Revelation 4 is John's account of what he saw, difficult as it must have been to express in the language of this world and in relation to limited human experience. It is a vision of God, the Almighty One, sitting on his throne and surrounded by his heavenly servants. The vision ends with a song of praise to God who created all things of his own will.

Here, and nowhere else, is the real key to understanding our world, the heart of the matter, the crux of the good news told to man. There is meaning because God exists, and he created all things.

Just as the book of Revelation provides us with insight into the heart of all creation, it also gives us a key to understanding the flow of human history. History is not just events, mere historical cause and effect. It is not a long list of dates in a textbook. Ultimately, history is the work of Christ, the Lord of history, and it unfolds itself because he acts within and into it.

A reading of Revelation 5 discloses this. We see Christ and the power of the Holy Spirit. Christ, the promised Messiah, is the Lamb "looking as if it had been slain." He is the

Lord who died on the cross and rose from the grave. He is with God and receives the scroll, the Book of Life. He takes the Book and opens it, removing the seals one by one, and gradually unveils human history.

All this is described in language that is difficult for men of the twentieth century to understand. John's language is symbolic, images taken from natural reality in order to describe a level of reality beyond the reach of man's sight or understanding. What John writes about is not just thoughts or fantasies.

Revelation seems indeed an obscure book, but it is less so for those who know the prophetic books of the Old Testament and are familiar with Jesus' prophecies of events to come. In this sense, Revelation is not a new book, for it adds nothing to the Bible that has not been mentioned elsewhere. Rather, it is a reminder that many of the things described by the prophets are still to happen, even though many prophecies have been fulfilled in the life, death, and resurrection of Christ. Revelation can be seen as a great collection of Old Testament quotations, using the same language and images. It shows everything in its proper perspective: history unfolding itself from the day Christ rose from the dead to later ascend into Heaven, on to the present, and then on again to the Last Judgment.

History is not a "nice story." Jesus himself spoke of wars, famines, and earthquakes to come. In Revelation we are told that he is to come in the midst of all these things, events that even in the heavenly realms are described as "woes" (Revelation 8:13). Christ is purifying the world, preparing it for the day when all things, even death, will be subjected to God's dominion (1 Corinthians 15:24ff.) and the new earth will come into being.

We stand in awe as we realize that all these great things—including the death and resurrection of God the Son—will have been necessary in order to bring about final victory over darkness and evil and the complete restoration of justice.

As awesome as this all sounds, it does not take place

without the involvement of men and their actions, whether great or small. The unseen world is inextricably intertwined with the natural world, and each has a significant effect on the other. Often we brush aside as unimportant the little sorrows and pains of life, as well as its good and positive moments. But the Bible assures us that they all have meaning.

In this book we shall consider our actions, our history, our culture, our creativity—the little deeds of little men and women, all incomplete and imperfect (Romans 8:20). Yet they are crucial and have their place in God's great scheme. We can sit down and think about our work, our calling, and know that it is real and full of significance. Our actions have far wider results than we could ever have imagined. We are called upon to play a role in an immense drama, in the great tribulations of our era, as well as in the little adventures and battles, whether spiritual or material. This is no game, but reality itself.

Part One: Being Christian in a Broken World

CHAPTER ONE

Man's Calling in God's Creation

GOD'S HAND IN HISTORY

There is indeed more to history than meets the eye. While it may be easy to go along with this proposition, it is frequently difficult to discern the "more." Pious believers often devaluate history by regarding it simply as the story of how God saves sinful men and women; others view history as a random sequence of events—human greed leading to violence and warfare. But the final truth about history goes deeper.

The Bible—especially the book of Revelation—offers a perspective on the whole of history. It shows God at work in creation and then in judgment, the warfare against him waged by the powers of evil under their prince, God's work of redemption and deliverance, and the assurance of a final victory in which his children will share.

Although there is this meaning to be discerned behind events, there is in the biblical view no ultimate duality, nothing Hegelian. History is one; within the "little" things that happen, God's great purposes are being fulfilled until finally his Kingdom will appear, unchallenged, untarnished. (First Corinthians 15:24-28 briefly tells the story.)

Within the theater of history, man is neither a puppet nor a passive spectator. Even if both the decisive victory and the final triumph must be acts of God, since weakness and sin disqualify man from such an achievement, nevertheless God, after his work of deliverance in the coming, death, and resurrection of his Son, calls man to action. God invites man to help prepare a new world in which all things will be unified in Christ (Ephesians 1:10).

Few people today take seriously an event at the beginning of history which has affected everything since—the Fall. Man, tempted to be like God, to be his own master, broke God's one basic commandment and set in motion a series of momentous events. Death came into the world. The creation, now cursed by God, became subject to futility (Romans 8:20). How little Christians have studied the implications of this curse.

Although they, quite rightly, study the meaning of God's grace, they fail to deal with issues like Ecclesiastes' description of the vanity of human activity. Yet despite all frustration, futility and suffering, our daily life still has meaning and is waiting to be set free from the bondage of decay (Romans 8:21).

Adam and Eve must have had an extremely limited understanding of the great things God prophesied in that ominous moment just after the Fall. Even today, sin and death distort our understanding of reality; as Paul says, we now see things in a "poor reflection" (1 Corinthians 13:12). Nevertheless, our hope is that one day we will come to full understanding.

All mankind awaits salvation from the curse, from the power of evil, from the futility of human work; we look forward to the fulfillment of the promise that all creation will one day be cleansed and liberated. Meanwhile, mankind is called to work. God's world is still there, and it is still our responsibility to till and keep it (Genesis 2:15). We are also to create, within the framework of our humanity.[1] It is for man to activate and realize, to discover and give form to the world's inherent potential.

This is all possible because, in spite of the curse, God also gave hope. The "seed of the woman" was to conquer the serpent, Satan. As history progressed, God made clear, both through his prophets and the work and teaching of Jesus, that it was Christ who was to be this "seed"; and although the serpent was to bruise his heel, the woman's seed would attain the victory.

Ever since God said that liberation would come through the seed of the woman, mankind has been looking to its offspring, the next generation, to overcome the results of the curse. Eve looked at Cain in this way: would he be the redeemer? Cain proved instead to be a murderer. Yet even Cain was not simply put aside, nor were his offspring deprived of their humanity. The cultural mandate, that all mankind was to develop and utilize this world, remained in force. God canceled neither his plans, nor his creation; he continues his great work of restoration. And although this must now be achieved the hard way, through suffering, pain and death, there is also the resurrection of Christ, making possible the resurrection of all who in him have become new men and women (Romans 6:8-11).

Thus the cultural task of mankind remains, but in history there have always been two ways of fulfilling this task, represented on the one hand by the line of Cain and Lamech, and on the other by the line of Seth and Enoch.

MAN'S WORK IN HISTORY

Cain and Lamech—Self-sufficient Man

Cain and Lamech are the forebears of all those throughout history who do things their own way, without reverence for the God who made them. We read of them in Genesis 4:17ff. In the activities of these men and their descendants we soon find a development: man discovers possibilities and gives them a specific form. This opening up of culture is the making of history. We read of the invention of shelter against sun and rain, of the beginning of animal husbandry, the beginning of music, and the use of tools. Man starts to make himself comfortable.

Lamech immediately begins to misuse these tools. He brags about his weapons. God had given Cain protection; but Lamech boasts that he can do even better, and uses his strength to take more than one woman. Already at the beginning of history we have sex and violence, in the line of Cain and Lamech, just as we find them today, described in the newspapers with their stories of crime and prostitution, or in books, theater, movies, and art—except that our "enlightened" age does these things even more powerfully than Lamech.

"Man himself; man through himself!" sings Lamech. His power and cunning will win. And because in his day sex also meant children, man would become strong and powerful through his children. Deliverance and freedom would come through man's seed. Such freedom, however, is the freedom of the strong, and means the enslavement of the weak—the weaker sex, those weaker in battle, or the economically and socially weak. Mankind thus begins to look for freedom, dreaming of a new world and a man-made salvation, to be achieved by the strong.

Man even begins to long for the unity of all mankind. After the Fall this unity had immediately been broken; there was the family of Adam and the family of Cain. Later, the breach between men became even greater with the episode of the Tower of Babel, which was, ironically, a desperate bid for unity. Hereafter, unity could be achieved only through power. The great empires of Babylon, Persia and Rome do indeed show a certain unity—a unity often brought about through the suppression and enslavement of many surrounding peoples. But these empires never achieve a true unity, for mankind is shattered. In spite of attractive principles and theories, unity rarely means more than that connections and relations can be established, however temporary or insubstantial.

Faith in Progress

As man strives for a better world, he chooses his own gods.

These gods are meant to make him great. A glance at any history book will show that one of the great driving forces in man is his faith in the god of progress. He believes that through his seed, progress will be achieved. Man tries to change man, either through ideas or through force, hoping for the emergence of a better world. He tries to change human systems, only to find that this also is not the solution. Still, in desperation, he goes on. Wars and revolutions, violence and suppression are the fruits of man's faith in progress. All too frequently sincere idealists are superseded by power-seekers who misuse even the best things to reach their own goals.

Meanwhile, in his quest for progress, man develops techniques and crafts, creates cities and works of art, thinks deeply about life, writes books, sings songs, and organizes his world into all kinds of systems. More and more he has learned to utilize the wealth of materials and the potential present in nature.

In themselves these things are not to be despised. The Bible never belittles beauty or refinement. It praises the beauty of the cities that are destroyed: Babylon, Nineveh, Tyre, and Sidon. Listen to the description in Ezekiel 27 and 28 of the wealth, the skill, the abundant goods of Tyre. We are certainly not encouraged to look upon these achievements with contempt. In fact, we are told to lament because they are gone, destroyed. Their wisdom was even greater than Daniel's (28:3). They were destroyed because Tyre was "filled with violence, and . . . sinned, . . . [its] heart became proud on account of [its] beauty, . . . [it] corrupted [its] wisdom because of [its] splendor. . . . By [its] many sins and dishonest trade [it] desecrated [its] sanctuaries" (28:16-18). Also (28:2) Tyre had said, "I am a god."

Man's Achievements

Who has not seen the treasures of those days and admired the skill of their artisans, the ability of their engineers, their development of trades and the work of their sculptors and painters! The great bulls with human heads which act as watchmen at the palace gates of ancient Mesopotamia are more awe-inspiring than reassuring (imagine what it was like to go through the gates of a tyrant's palace!), but they do testify to a great culture. They achieved something worthy of respect. But precisely because such beautiful things were used to support tyranny and the lust for power, they seem the more horrible.

Throughout history, many discoveries and techniques—the "opened potentiality"—are handed down from one generation to the next. We still employ many of them today. It is sin which turns these good things into a curse, when they are used to serve the Moloch of progress.

We need not discuss our own era, with its great achievements in micro- and macro-physics, its superior technological developments—and yet inner decay, a growing number of dictators, endless abuse of power, perhaps even less by states than by vast international companies, which are demonic in their anonymous greed, their uncontrollable activities for which no one seems to be responsible. But the understanding that both the gods and man are dead is something new, and a sign that history is hastening to its end.

Our era is characterized by a spiritual wasteland, such confusion as has possibly never before existed in history. Christianity has been cast aside. Secularization is the key-word of our age, in spite of the many who are searching for another religion or myth to live by. Society itself is held to be neutral. We talk about a "pluralistic society" in which everyone holds private views which have no further meaning or impact on public life. At least, that is what one would lead us to think.

Revolution

Never before in history has there been such a widespread belief that revolution is positive, that by violent change a new world can be brought in. Already during the French

Revolution—the first in a long line—the revolutionaries felt this and introduced a new time scheme beginning with year 1 of the Revolution. The fact that this scheme was so short-lived proves that the Revolution in the end did not achieve its goals. Yet man returns again and again to this false hope. Young people today are caught up more than ever in these expectations; this is their ideology. They want to change mankind by changing the structures of society—mainly the economic and social structures. For them, man is defined not in relation to his gods, or to God himself, but by his place within an economic and social order.

Revolutionaries cannot wait for changes to come gradually. They want immediate results, trying to achieve equality by eliminating those who stand in their way. Certainly we would agree with them that all men are equal, but we mean equality before God and before the law. Truth and beauty are also the same for everybody. Revolutionaries, however, extend these truths into a demand that power should be given to the lower classes in order to achieve equal power and wealth—equality in everything! To achieve their ideal, they are even prepared to sacrifice individual freedom. Too often in reality this has meant that everyone was equally suppressed by a tyrant or dictator.

Revolutions are unhappy periods, times of uncertainty and lawlessness in which more is destroyed than built up. In a way, they are a sickness of humanity. Sometimes they are caused by the wrongdoings of the ruling classes, by unacceptable differences between wealth and poverty, and the suppression of those who are economically and socially weaker. During revolutionary periods, everyone looks forward to the time when all will be settled and life will return to "normal." Sometimes—even often perhaps—something *is* achieved in a revolution. We must not think, however, as the present generation does, that this is the direct fruit of revolution; at best, the revolution paved the way so that these new gains could be realized. A certain development had come so far, until greed or conservatism or lack of concern blocked the way. Then revolution gave it a chance.

If a person is sick, he may have a crisis, followed by a gradual restoration to health. The healing is not the result of the crisis itself, but of the body's driving out the poisons that have been afflicting it. After the French Revolution, for example, more power went to the middle classes, and in general freedom was increased and oppression reduced. No one would deny that these things were positive. But because the Revolution was also a time of terror, and later of dictatorship, these beneficial changes were almost halted. Such things happen because revolutionary man has no patience to bear burdens, nor to wait for God to act. He wants immediate results.

Besides the crises of revolution, there are also what I would call the fevers of growth. While they may include some marks of revolution, they are essentially times of heightened creativity. One example is the birth of the Dutch nation, which freed Protestantism and liberated the nation from the very conservative force of Spain. Or consider the birth of the United States of America: growth and development had come to the point that the American colonies were now to be accepted as equal to the mother country, not colonies anymore. But the Old World did not understand, and the result was the War of Independence.

Seth and Enoch—Salt in a Decaying World

Growth

In the line of Seth and Enoch, as in that of Cain and Lamech, we also find development and change. But here is no dream of bringing about a new world through revolution or man's endeavor. The children of God are called, along with the rest of mankind, to work towards the unfolding and realization of this world's potential. But they are given the added understanding that in the time between the Fall and the return of Christ, nothing good can be achieved without at the same time taking into account sin and its results. We can accomplish nothing without a continual battle against evil. Christians are called to be the salt of the earth, to preserve and add flavor to what is good, and to bring a measure of healing where man is sick and broken.

Alas, the church has too often ignored the suffering and oppression of the poor, and neglected her calling to help the needy and sick. We are to work concretely for peace and freedom. The message of the prophets has always been: Repent! Turn back to the Lord, and show that you love him. Do not just offer sacrifice and praise, but *do* the truth (John 3:21). What does the Lord require of us but to "act justly and to love mercy and to walk humbly with [our] God" (Micah 6:8).

Here one finds a basis for unity—the communion of saints. Here the redemption of the world begins. Although even here sin abounds, and no Christian can say that Christianity as such will bring in the new world, still much good has been achieved. Many of the world's wounds have been healed through the sacrificial lives of thousands of saints—saints in the sense used by Paul and others, saints because their sins were forgiven by the Lord, and because they achieved something through the renewing power of Christ's work.

In the line of Seth and Enoch, the Lord has sent great men to show the way: Moses, Elijah, David, Daniel, the apostles, Augustine, Luther, Calvin, and many more. There have also been great scientists and artists. And although even the best works of all these men are tinged with sin, our Western culture owes them a great debt—the West which is presently in a state of decay because people have fallen away from God, but where we still find laws requiring monogamy, and laws which presuppose charity and trustworthiness.

Science too was a fruit of Christianity, which saw nature as separate from the God who had created it, and therefore open to exploration. And in the seventeenth century, when there was a Christian consensus, art in northern Europe reached a peak that has never been surpassed. The art of that century has a richness and technical brilliance yet to be fully investigated, even though our museums are full of "old masters" and many books have already been devoted to them. People may be critical of all these achievements, but they usually use as their measuring rod Christian ethics and Christian standards, thus paradoxically demonstrating the depth of Christian influence.

As we have seen, the line of Seth and Enoch does look for development and renewal; but unlike the other line of humanity, it realizes that these things must come through a gradual *growth*.

Although the line of Cain and the line of Seth work so differently, both are working within the same framework of God's creation, towards the goal of realizing its potential and thus making it a good home for mankind, ultimately overcoming evil and the curse. Both lines form part of the same humanity with the same basic calling.

Renewal

Ultimately, complete redemption from evil will come with the judgment of God, when the seals of the Book of Life are opened, letting loose all the woes described in Revelation. Meanwhile, the work of developing and maintaining the world is often done mainly by the people of the line of Cain and Lamech. That does not mean that the line of Seth and Enoch is to withdraw from participation in the world, as will be clear further on. But the special task of the line of Seth and Enoch is to be "salting salt" (Matthew 5:13, my rendering). Salt is used to preserve, or at least to postpone decay and corruption. Christians are called to show by their words and their lives that God exists and that Christ is his Son. Saltless Christianity will be thrown aside. Judgment begins with the church (1 Peter 4:17), and anyone who becomes a Christian just to have a kind of supreme insurance policy is badly mistaken! Not those who say "Lord, Lord" will inherit the Kingdom of Heaven, but those who actively love God and their neighbors (Matthew 25:31ff.).

Christ did not die simply to make men Christians. That is not enough; his work is too great. He died so that we might be human, living and acting in a human way, as God originally made us to live, in love and freedom. Christ is not just the Redeemer of the Christians, nor the guru for those who follow his cult, nor the Lord of "our faith"—we should not have faith in faith—but he came to redeem and restore the whole creation, and to be its supreme Judge.

The decay we see around us can be halted only when with God's help and a life of prayer we appropriate the power of Christ's resurrection to live as renewed human beings (Romans 6). God's call to "Seek righteousness, seek humility" (Zephaniah 2:3) is certainly not a matter of conquering the world for God, but rather of beginning, ourselves, to walk in obedience.

Real fruit in the Christian's life can only be achieved as we are sanctified through Christ's work. Redemption does not merely mean a "spiritual" blessing, something which happens to our soul so that we feel the Lord close to us. Of course, the Lord *can* be near his people, answering their prayers, and can be present with them in a special way when they are persecuted (Luke 21:12ff.). He forgives their sins and leads them in his way by the Holy Spirit. But these graces are not to be an end in themselves. They encourage those who are working in his Kingdom, helping them to go on doing the things he told them to do in this world. Freedom in the midst of this world's troubles, and miracles of God's intervention can have meaning only within the context of sacrificial obedience to him, doing as well as hearing the word (James 1:22).

Humility is the key-word. Power, riches, greatness are not ends in the Christian's life, nor even means. Christ is our example: born in a manger, surrounded by lowly people, and growing up in a place remote from the cultural centers of his time. His life and work were of the same quality, sacrifice and service—washing others' feet! His end was death on the cross. What appeared to be weakness was his triumph! We must never confuse humility with softness and passivity, for no weakling could have denounced the Pharisees or opposed hypocrisy, corruption and dishonesty as Jesus did.

Christ's death was not a theological proposition or a statement of creed. It was and is reality, the center of history, for in Christ God redeemed the world, conquering sin and death. Christ's death is the fulfillment of all history, and the realization of all potential, all promises.

Our Common Humanity

Looking back over so many thousands of years, we must acknowledge that something has been achieved. Hygiene, comfort, freedom, wealth and justice have been attained by men, although they are so precarious and even scarce that they have to be continuously defended.

Human accomplishments are important, even if they are not absolute, and they certainly form part of God's plan for a great future. The task to subdue the earth and have dominion over all creatures (Genesis 1:28; 9:1, 2) has been carried out, if only partially, and in spite of sin, pain, sorrow, and tears.

The question, however, is often asked: how is it possible for an unbeliever, a non-Christian, to do works that are both good in themselves (even though done by sinful man) and at the same time acceptable to a Christian, who is a child of God? An answer is often given in terms of "common grace," suggesting that God gives a special kind of grace, grace in a general sense, so that good things are possible. This common grace is sharply distinguished from particular grace, through which the Christian gains salvation, the forgiveness of sin, and the power to do good.

I feel that this is a wrong question, leading to a wrong answer. The nonbeliever is not a devil, devoid of the possibility of doing any good, even if he is a sinful man. He is above all a human being who may or may not see that he needs salvation. He certainly wishes for a good and fine world, even though he may have only a distorted idea of what this means.

Since the nonbeliever does not accept God as his Savior, and since he wants to make a better world in his own strength and wisdom, he may cling to strange beliefs or an unfounded optimism. But he is not master of God's creation. His insights do not constitute reality, although they color his achievements and his attempts to make a better world. Reality remains as it is. If man wants to achieve something lasting, he must capitulate to reality and its God-given structures, and this may cause him either pain or joy. We cannot call it grace, unless we call it grace that God has not yet removed the unbeliever from this world, as not belonging here. This will happen only at the end of history, when the rebel will experience a second death, and be denied a place in the new earth.

The non-Christian is still man, in the full sense of the word. Even if sinful, he can work in this world and create things of value and intrinsic quality. (And, just as with a Christian, sin will mar all he does.) If he is a philosopher and wants people to hear him, he must say something sensible, since no one cares to listen to nonsense (this is part of the capitulation to reality). If he is an artist, his art must be beautiful, or he will run into problems and his art will become a strange phenomenon remote from reality—something almost unknown in history apart from modern art. The politician, too, must at least try to deal with actual problems and work for a just economic situation; otherwise he will be a tyrant who constantly lives in fear of revolt. Likewise, the tradesman must carry on his business with some honesty and some positive rules, or he soon will have lost all his customers!

There *is* a deep difference between Christians and non-Christians, but we must not look for it in the wrong place. The difference lies ultimately in man's basic attitude, his hope, and his understanding of his task. But when it comes to any specific activity, the Christian may be foolish and sinful and the unbeliever wise and right. Essentially, the Christian and the non-Christian are traveling down totally different roads, but as humans living in the same created world and in the same history, their differences may be less black and white. That means we can truly communicate with each other.

Summary—No Shortcuts

The road to complete fulfillment of the goals of creation is a long one. God chose the road of growth and progress—giving man creativity and the freedom to be his co-worker. Having made man in his own image, he has called him to participate in a process which leads him to eternal life. It is a way of obedience, marked by love, freedom, truth, justice, and beauty.

The devil has always preferred shortcuts: You can have it now; be like God; just eat the fruit. We all know what happened. The devil presented Christ with the same temptation in the desert (Luke 4): Bow down before me, and you will be Lord over this earth. But Jesus knew that God's way to Lordship led through suffering—a longer but more certain road.

When man ate from the tree of knowledge, he did get to know good and evil. God did not change his plans because of this, but now the road has become cursed, a way of suffering, pain and death (Genesis 3:15, 23). There is also now the enmity between the seed of the woman and the seed of the serpent, the clash between good and evil. History has become a long story of violence and war, injustice and revolutions, but also of idealism and good deeds. Inseparably entangled in a complex knot, the seed of the woman and the seed of the serpent together make history. Those who, with Cain's offspring, try to take the shortcut of revolution, to have it all now, inflict deep wounds which make the world ugly and end in new sorrows. Man cannot be his own redeemer, and if he rejects God's reign he may find himself bowed under a rod of iron.

God will bring the redemption man himself can never achieve. Meanwhile, we are to go on with our human task, accepting suffering and the less-than-perfect. In this way, although we may not understand it, we will be working toward the fulfillment of God's purposes.

FREEDOM AND AUTHORITY

Unless man is prepared to accept chaos, he must achieve some agreement about objectives, a certain unity. We call this a consensus: moral aims and laws to strive for which constitute a social and political basis for society. The weaker these become, as we see happening today, the less freedom there is, and the greater the threat of chaos. Witness, for example, the rising crime rate in our big cities, and the resulting need for caution which hinders our freedom to go where we like.

Because it is a dream to think all men are good and working towards identical objectives, God in his wisdom has given us the State to punish the criminal, to preserve public security, and to uphold justice in relationships between people. The world needs some power that possesses authority, as Paul makes clear (Romans 13:1ff.).

Authority Re-evaluated—the Position of Women

Immediately after the Fall, God instituted authority. He placed the man over the woman, and told her that she was to look to him as the master. The man was to protect the woman and work to provide for her. The man became ruler over the woman, over his offspring, over nature. The woman was to help the man and be the mother of his children. The Fall thus necessitated some loss of freedom, just as it brought suffering into the world.

These words in Genesis, however, were not a command or a law; they merely stated a fact that was henceforth to color the reality of man and woman. The Christian should try to soften this reality and make the burden lighter; no man has the right to be a hard taskmaster, and women were not intended to be a kind of cattle. Men, however, being the more powerful, often behaved as the Marquis de Sade was later to preach, using their superior physical strength to gratify all their personal whims.

The biblical position is very different. In its history of the position of women, we have an excellent example of the meaning of growth, as opposed to revolution. As early as the laws of Moses we find many rules governing the position of women, laws in which there is no revolution, no immediate break with the past or present practices of society. But inherent in all these God-given laws is a growing tendency towards monogamous marriage and a better position for women.

These things cannot, however, be enforced in a day, at one stroke. Real change takes time, for it involves not only outward obedience to a law, but a change of mentality and attitude. Without an altered mentality, sinful men will only find ways to circumvent the laws and make the situation even worse.

After the law of Moses, the New Testament brought more changes along the road to more freedom for women. Today in the Western world monogamy is the law. In many Muslim countries, and elsewhere where people follow the ways of the West, women have been gaining more freedom, even if the end has not yet been reached.

However, when women try to force the pace of emancipation in a revolutionary manner, it often makes things worse. The women's liberation movement has turned the gains of the past, in which women were gradually gaining more equality, into a battle of the sexes. Instead of the closeness and unity between men and women, involving a recognition of the wonderful diversity each has received by creation, we have hatred. Women begin to act in an ugly way, and are no longer themselves because imitating men.

Today, as Christianity is slowly pushed aside, we see a gradual loss of those values which began to be realized in the laws of Moses. The position of women is threatened; free love and permissiveness abound, and easier divorce laws are leading to greater breakdown of marriages. It is women who will suffer most from all this.

I am not of course suggesting a return to the laws of Moses; that would be retreating to a bygone position. We must see those laws as pointers, to prevent an even further retreat! Ours is the long way, the way of patience and perhaps of suffering, as we defend what has been realized. But this gradual process has had great results. Even today, despite all attempts to undo the process, we find that these ideas and principles are deeply engrained in people's minds and deteriorate only very slowly. Monogamy is still the rule. Women are still safeguarded from the evil of men.

Authority's Rightful Place

As we have seen in the position of women, when the Bible teaches us to accept authority, it never means that the bearer of it can do as he likes. His authority is always related to God's commands. A person in authority must not say, "Do what I say," but rather, "This is the norm or rule, and I am bound to it as well."

The world still needs authority and protection. Injustice and chaos can result from too much equality. The family, for instance, is important and so is the rule of obedience to parents! That the new psychologically-oriented teaching methods have said otherwise is one reason that we currently have a crisis of authority in the world. On the other hand, we must be very careful that our view of authority does not degenerate to the relationship between a ruler and his slaves.

We live, then, in a revolutionary era. There is socialist egalitarianism which would turn man's rightful equality before God and the law into a demand for equality in all respects—even going so far as to bypass the great differences between men and women. There is women's lib. There is the call for a new democracy, which is often anarchy, recognizing no authority whatsoever. And there is also Marxism with its Utopian idea of making a better world through revolution, but it has brought tyranny, glossed over with the promise of a better world later, "for your children"!

THE "EASY-CHAIR MENTALITY"

During the Enlightenment a new quest, a new mentality, started to become part of man's thinking. We may call it the "easy-chair mentality." I hit upon this expression when I noticed that before the eighteenth century, easy chairs were never made, not even for the very rich. The easy chair is not a feat of modern technology; mankind could have made it in the distant past, but nobody did. The easy chair is the result of a new mentality that demands all ease, all comfort now. Maybe in the past men accepted discomfort too easily. Perhaps in an almost fatalistic way they did not try to overcome the cold, the lack of water, the poor accommodation, and the slow means of travel. We certainly cannot object to the quest for more comfort, running hot and cold water, a good heating system, and improved roads and transport; we surely would not put up with the services offered in the ages before the Enlightenment. As human beings we are participants in the development of these new conveniences, and as Christians we have no reason to say no to them.

But we should say no to the *mentality* that is involved; it sometimes drives man on too far, into absurdity. The developments themselves may be legitimate, but sometimes they cost too much. We must establish priorities; to insist on the good things here and now, while others suffer poverty and live far below our level of comfort, makes us unjust, overdemanding, and even cruel.

This is the mentality which says everything that can be done *should* be done. If we can build planes that go slightly faster (even if they cause more pollution and more noise), then we ought to have them—even if no one really needs them! We say, "It's absolutely essential," which often means, "We want to have it, and we won't wait, even if social evils are the result." Or we insist that we must remain competitive in the world market. But may not competition itself sometimes be evil?

As long ago as 1831, Carlyle accurately described this mentality in *Sartor Resartus:* "Man's Unhappiness as I construe, comes of his Greatness; it is because there is an Infinite in him, which with all his cunning he cannot quite bury under the Finite. Will the whole Finance Ministers and Upholsterers and Confectioners of modern Europe undertake, in joint-stock company, to make one Shoeblack HAPPY? They cannot accomplish it, above an hour or two; for the Shoeblack also has a Soul quite other than his Stomach, and would require, if you consider it, for his permanent satisfaction and saturation, simply this allotment, no more, and no less: *God's Infinite Universe altogether to himself,* therein to enjoy infinitely, and fill every wish as fast as it rose."[2] I think Carlyle is right. But that means that the shoeblack is doing the same foolish thing as man did at the Fall, wanting to be like God, wanting in fact to be a god himself—in order to get his wishes fulfilled.

Ours is the age of the instantaneous. The advertisements cry, "Take this pill for instant relief!" The generation of the sixties was sometimes called the "now generation." If they bumped up against a wall of reality which did not obey their whims, then they fell back into apathy, despairing because their desires could not be met immediately. They had no patience, certainly not the patience of waiting on the Lord.

Christians too have been infected with this mentality. We have all the comforts, life is easy, and every wish can be fulfilled—if we belong to the happy rich. Our economy has done so much to make everyone wealthy, more wealthy even than the kings of old, whose palaces could not compete with our bungalows in comfort. We have all this. But not everything is in our hands. Some things are beyond our control: good health, a happy marriage, and a sense of achievement. So we call on the Lord and ask him to provide them for us, as if he were a magician on a string—our string!

How often people have asked me what is meant by "answer to prayer." In probing the questioners, I have found that they are often looking for the immediate fulfillment of wishes beyond their power. I have also often been asked what the "fear of the Lord" means. There may indeed be a lack of clarity in communication here, as the word "fear" in this sense has become obsolete. But the question also shows that man today has lost the understanding of a great God Almighty who commands our awe and wonder. We find it difficult to bow deeply before the Supreme God and say, "Thy will be done." Too often we have made Christianity into a happiness system, guaranteeing success the easy way, with God there in his power to fill in the gaps.

Science

Modern science also has been affected by this mentality. In its early phase, science developed because people wanted to understand the world in which they lived, and to use this knowledge for practical purposes. In the words of Susanne K. Langer: "Practical gain, dominion over nature, were [Science's] early motives; its motives were intellectual, they lay in the restless desire of an ever imaginative mind to exploit the possibilities of the factual world as a field for constructive thought."

This attitude changed with the new secularized mentality of the eighteenth century. Now science became two things. First, it was a way of knowing things, or rather the *only* way of knowing things, whether natural or human. Second, science began to try to take control of all things for man's own benefit. Says Langer: "We know that knowledge is power, that it is something more than mental satisfaction, that it enables us to use the facts of life and the secrets of nature for human benefit. Knowledge makes us able to do things, and so add to the sum of human well-being."

Nowadays we enter our home, turn on a switch, and billions of electrons move at the fastest possible speed to give us light. This can be the result of a legitimate desire to know facts in order to put them to use, possible only if we ourselves submit to nature and its laws. But we can go too far, and want too much, in the process becoming natural facts ourselves, caught in the laws of nature and the laws controlling society and economy.

Political-economic Systems

Like science, Marxism has also fallen into the easy-chair mentality. It too looks for a way to force nature to serve man. And man himself is forced into subjection to a social-economic order which completely rules his behavior and even his thinking. Man wants to rule nature, but he has lost his status as a steward, as described in Genesis 1:28ff. and Genesis 2:15. As a result, nature is against man, to be subdued almost as an enemy.

Socialism, the offspring of Marxism, has been much more fruitful, because it accepts that this world has to change slowly if it is to change at all. It has done much good in its concern for the economically weaker. Socialism tends, however, to overstress the economic, and assumes too readily that happiness can be achieved through centralized plans, which leave too little freedom to the individual. It is too egalitarian, seeking to make all men the same, at least in the economic sense.

Even if the Marxist or the socialist thinks that Christianity has been too slow, and has accepted pain and inconvenience too easily, he must recognize that many of his ideas and ideals have their roots in Christianity. In a way, these are Christian heresies, claiming that the benefits they seek can be had by human endeavor, without God. Often they are anti-God, and certainly anti-Christian.

In the Western world, capitalism also continues to be very strong. With its laissez-faire, laissez-aller principles, its belief in free enterprise and the positive aspects of competition, it too assigns too great a priority to the economic side of life. In fact, it has called into being the bourgeois way of life. Capitalism in itself is certainly not Christian, and has caused many of the injustices we see today. It too has been colored by the easy-chair mentality.

Our Western pluralistic society assumes religion to be irrelevant to our public life, to political, social and economic reality. While this view of religion as a field in which the individual must decide for himself offers Christians valuable freedom, we must not fall into the trap of leaving this world to be run by the principles of Cain, while we carry on our private lives as the line of Seth. Not only does such behavior imply a restricted view of God; it will not work. We cannot continue to enjoy the fruits of a long process in which Christianity has played a decisive role if the foundation of our world order, including morality, becomes divorced from obedience to God. We simply cannot live our daily lives in a closed world order, totally naturalistic and without God, and then on Sunday proclaim that the world is open and that God and his Kingdom are true realities; such a position is schizophrenic. We are one, and the world is one.

THE CHRISTIAN'S TASK

Preservation of the World

Christians must accept the good things that have been done by the line of Cain and Lamech. Humanity has been given a great responsibility, in the interests of a great future. We must beware of taking judgment on these matters into our own hands (Romans 12:19; 1 Corinthians 5:13). The Christian's task is not to change the world—wonderful as this would be if it led to better morals, better justice, better management of the world's resources—but primarily to keep the world from decay and corruption, evil and suppression.

The Christian lives in tension. On the one hand, knowing that man is sinful, he does not expect a Utopia. He accepts the world as it is after the Fall, knowing that it is unnatural, subject to pain and death and crying out for removal of the curse. He knows that only Christ can bring renewal. On the other hand, the Christian can never merely accept this malfunctioning, this pain and suffering. He may never abandon his duty, but is called to follow Christ's example, to relieve or fight the effects of evil. In this sense the Christian is a protester, but his is a protest in love. It takes wisdom and love to know when to accept the less than perfect, and when to press on for something better.

The Christian cannot be a revolutionary. The Bible teaches us to be patient and not to take up the sword. While there may be some exceptions, they must be very strong in order to justify violence.[3] Christians are not even to assassinate tyrants; think of David, who in spite of a unique opportunity, refused to kill Saul (1 Samuel 24). Both the Bible and experience teach that violence only breeds more violence. Christians should be peacemakers, though never of a "peace at all costs," which leads to evil and oppression.

If Christians want to draw others to accept Christ, they must demonstrate what it means to be a child of God. A child of God is not someone who is always happy and content and without psychological problems. He is not someone who refrains from looking at bad things, letting the world go its own way because he believes it is rotten anyway. Nor should he be someone who defends the Establishment as such, just for the sake of peace (Jeremiah 6:13-15).

Far from retreating into a kind of Christian subculture, leaving the world to its evil, Christians not only can, but *must* take part in the world's activity. This could even be called pre-evangelism; it is indeed the only way that evangelism itself can ever be really fruitful. It means doing our work with honesty and care, excelling where possible, never cheating, never letting the ends justify the means, being always responsible and reliable.

Above all, our involvement in the world means perseverance. If we want to work towards a change in the right direction, we must realize that it cannot be done by one person, nor in a few years. It is an endless task for all Christians in all ages. Only in this way can God use us. Our work will not be in vain, even when we have no hope of seeing results in the near future, and when we must wait to see fulfillment later, perhaps only on the new earth.

Christians should be better than other men and women, not to call attention to themselves, but because they have such a great God. Their sanctification must be evident in the fruits of the Spirit. Not that Christian men and women are to work for success and prestige, the world's criteria of greatness. Often they will be second-rate in the eyes of the world, just because being "salting salt" takes so much energy!

CHAPTER TWO

The Christian in His Culture

"CHRISTIANITY AND CULTURE"— A FALSE DICHOTOMY

There is no shortage of books on Christianity and culture. Unfortunately, reading them often tends to leave one with a sense of dissatisfaction, as if the most important aspect of the subject had not even been touched upon. In spite of every effort to show their interrelatedness, Christianity and culture have remained alien to each other. Is it perhaps the very plan of most of these books, articles, or lectures that is to blame? First comes a beautiful, clear definition of Christianity, then a definition of culture. Finally there is an attempt to confront the two, to unify them, or set them over against each other. The titles of the books highlight the problem, taking as they do the form, "Christianity and . . . (Science . . . Economics . . . Art)."

Have we been making a mistake? Can an abstraction like "Christianity" really have any meaning? Might it not be better just to consider Christians, weak and strong, profound and superficial, who are thinking and working? Culture also can be understood in these terms, rather than by means of an abstract definition. Our attempts to relate Christianity and culture sometimes fail precisely because we have mistakenly thought of them as separated from the beginning.

The problem of Christianity and culture has also often been approached historically, in an attempt to show how people acted in different ways at different times. This approach is useful, and helps us to see what a living faith meant in the struggles of a particular period. But sometimes we become too critical when we do this, and in pointing out a period's shortcomings, as for example the asceticism of the Middle Ages, we fail to do justice to the good that was also present. This happens because standing, as we do, at a distance, we see very easily how "they" were children of their times; yet, unaware of the difficulties they faced, we become overly conscious of their failures, and of what we—from our viewpoint—see as shortcomings. On the other hand, in studying a period when God gave his blessing there is the danger that we may misapply its attainments to reinforce or defend our own personal views. There is thus the very real danger of ending up with self-imposed problems or hasty conclusions unrelated to past or present reality.

DEFINING "CULTURE"

The Christian's Environment

There are two ways of discussing Christianity and culture. First we may consider the attitude that the individual Christian and the Christian community should adopt towards the surrounding non-Christian culture. This problem is met where Christians live in a world guided by consciously non- or anti-Christian principles, as in Russia; or one that is not consciously anti-Christian—such as the pagan world—where nevertheless the norms and ethics of life are different from those of Scripture. An issue that arose in such a situation was dealt with by Paul when he discussed the problem of eating meat that had been offered to pagan gods.

Wherever the gospel has been preached and taken root, it has necessarily involved the demythologizing of the pagan gods, exposing them to be no gods at all, or perhaps only impersonal forces like those of nature. Instances of such demythologizing in the Bible include the story of the god of the Philistines who fell to the ground when the ark was brought into his temple, or the words of Isaiah declaring the folly of a man's bowing before something which he himself has made (Isaiah 40:19ff.; 44:9ff.). Christianity has liberated the world, by demonstrating that all things—even the highest and strongest—are the creation of God. In this sense, Genesis 1 is the greatest liberating force in all history.

However, in any culture where Christianity has been preached, exposing the old gods as false, we must expect to find any subsequent decline of faith accompanied by secularization. This is the special problem of the Christian living in a world where Christianity is the nominally accepted standard, but people no longer live accordingly. God's world, his creation, remains, but people simply pass him by and ignore his life-giving words. The Christian's position in such an environment is difficult. What can he accept? Where should he draw the line? Clearly he must not take part in the sins of the culture that surrounds him. But what is the difference between a man who simply lives an autonomous life, and one who commits outright sin, deliberately disobeying one of God's clear commands? The Christian can share neither of these lifestyles. We must realize that although Christianity has an ethic, it is not in the first place an ethic. The rightness or wrongness of our way of life is to be measured against this principle: Love God, and accept his Son as the Savior.

The Christian's Activities

The second way to consider the relationship between Christianity and culture is to examine what Christianity itself produces. Has a specifically Christian culture been produced? Is this something Christians should attempt?

At this point we should try to formulate a definition of the term "culture." Over the last few centuries a restricted use of the word has been adopted, restricting it to the arts and the world of scholarship. This narrow application grows out of the inherent dualism of our culture. On the one hand are the strong forces of science and technology, which men today do not think of as culture, but simply as life and reality. On the other hand are scholarship and the *fine* arts: music, poetry, painting—interesting perhaps, but of little real consequence. (Maybe even religion belongs here.) Culture then becomes only an embellishment of life—an ornament, possibly even an enrichment, but never a necessity.

How far Christianity since the eighteenth century has reinforced this idea would be difficult to say. All too often it has looked on what is now called culture as something superfluous or even dangerous. At the same time, it has accepted modern science and technology with great naiveté as "neutral ground." Christians have too easily left the field of scholarship and the fine arts when they found that here the forces of unbelief were very active, forgetting that it is precisely at the front line that one has to engage the enemy. Consequently in some of these fields Christianity has relinquished almost all influence—for example, in the visual arts—and non-Christian ideas have found an almost undisputed freedom of expression. This has happened not only in the fine arts, literature and philosophy, but also in "entertainment"—films and television and the mass media in general. Thus the non-Christian mentality, world-view, and lifestyle have had such a powerful influence that people speak today of living in a "post-Christian era." Certainly the influence of Christianity has waned.

The term "culture," however, should not be restricted to intellectual and aesthetic pursuits. Such a dualism underlies the disharmony of our modern civilization. Life should be one, and culture is simply the creation of life's forms, customs, and institutions, as well as our utilization of nature and its resources. When a farmer cultivates, his methods and tools are all part of culture. When a composer writes a song, that is also culture. He chooses sounds and expresses ideas, creating a form whereby people can express themselves. As the popular song of the thirties said, "Without a song, there ain't no love at all."

Man is a creature, and has his own place within God's creation. There are innumerable areas in which he may be occupied: language and music, but also laws, liturgy, and economic systems. Involvement in these is inescapable, for man is a cultural being. If he has instincts at all, they are only very weak; his life is far from being predetermined like that of the animals. Man must build himself a home, grow his own food, and develop cooking methods. Also, he needs to find patterns for social intercourse. Whether people express their love for one another, demonstrate politeness or friendship, or assume roles in a hierarchical order, they do all these things within the special forms and customs which are part of culture.

Adam and Eve already set the pattern long ago. Adam gave everything a name and soon, after the Fall, both he and Eve were making clothes. Later on, script was developed in order to write, including our Bible.

THE CHRISTIAN'S PARTICIPATION IN CULTURE

Involvement Unavoidable

Christians should not disdain participation in culture. It may sound pious to say that the way we sing is not important, but to me it is almost the same as despising God. If one loves him, should one not try to sing good songs with good tunes? Moreover, to sing badly, for whatever reason, is also culture, even if only poor culture. For the Christian to make a duality in his life between on the one hand his spirituality and faith, and on the other the "neutral," more or less a-Christian activity of his daily experience, is to impoverish his existence. It denies God sovereignty over a large part of one's life and creates a dichotomy that is dangerous to our spirituality.

Asceticism, which entails becoming a hermit and escaping from the "world" and "culture" into a cave in the desert, should itself be recognized as a pattern of culture. In the early Christian era, this attitude led to the rise of the monasteries. In trying to save itself from "the world," the church avoided all cultural activity. This may explain why it was so long before the masses of "lay-people" became properly educated, and the rough world of the Dark Ages was replaced by something more refined and beautiful. Perhaps it was precisely because of this dualism in the mentality of the Christians that the new non-ecclesiastical culture—the Renaissance—which emerged at the end of the Middle Ages was so secularized. I say perhaps, because this is a complex matter about which I hesitate to make sweeping statements. But we can never totally avoid being cultured and creative beings; it is inherent to our humanity.

Christianity, or at any rate the Christian community, when it is small or its principles greatly at variance with those of the surrounding culture, is bound to develop a kind of subculture. I do not think we should be afraid of this; it is almost unavoidable. Yet we should also not see it as an ideal, and be content just to cultivate our own little garden. The Christian community should never behave as a "we-group" or an "in-group." It should not be proud of its lifestyle, its forms of worship, its ways of speaking or singing, for non-Christians may see it as odd, old-fashioned, and maybe even incomprehensible. Instead, Christians should always be open towards the world around them, and maintain contact with their contemporaries. The church should never be a closed community, removed from the world; after all, the mark of the world will always be within it, and may even manifest itself in the sin of pride!

New Creatures in Babel

Many of the problems which arise when we discuss the relationship between Christianity and culture come from treating them as separate entities; others result from confusing two different questions. The question of the place of a Christian in a non-Christian world is a very different one from the question of the attitude of the Christian towards living creatively. In the second case, the only legitimate question is: *How* can it be done? How can we creatively express our faith, our hopes and principles, our perspective on life? How does the Lord want us to work, think, create, and live?

Even in the early church there was already confusion about the two approaches to the relationship between Christianity and culture. The great question then was whether or not Christians should affirm solidarity with the surrounding culture. The Christians of those days, and particularly the more refined members of the upper classes, were raised and educated in the thought-patterns of Graeco-Roman civilization. For them, the question was how to regard this great culture, and particularly the philosophy which expressed its basic principles.

Two answers were formulated, in the words of Popma: "(1) a more synthetic one, which acknowledges elements of truth in Greek philosophy, and wants to make use of them, and (2) an antithetic attitude which condemns philosophy and the whole of pagan culture, and which considers a training in Greek philosophy to be useless, and even dangerous for a Christian."[1]

Those who accepted the first position found, in one way or another, that their understanding of the Bible became colored by the philosophical insights of Plato and others. They laid themselves open to the criticism that their thoughts at some points were more like a pagan's than obedience to Scripture should allow. "Both for our understanding of Philo's theology, and our understanding of Clement's and Origen's estimation of culture, it is of the greatest importance to recognize that the syntheses of the latter, which favor cultural solidarity, are based on a purely pagan religious basic idea."[2]

However, if we look at those who opposed this solidarity and who rejected classical culture, we see that they, perhaps even more than the others, made a synthesis with classical culture and were thus working from non-Christian principles. To quote Popma again: "Tatian has been struck by the Word-revelation, he has come to believe in Christ. . . . For him, that involves an evaluation of culture characterized by extreme opposition to cultural solidarity. He must have failed to realize altogether that in this way he was actually engaged in bringing about a synthesis. As is evident from his preserved writings, Tatian remained faithful to the subtleties of rhetorical training, and, in addition, his estimation of culture clearly betrays the Cynic marks of contempt for the world."[3] (The Cynics were a Greek philosophical school, of which Diogenes of Sinope has become the most famous figure, who held all culture, laws, customs, etc. in utter contempt.) As the attitude of these early Christian church leaders has strongly influenced Christian thought through the ages, it is not surprising to see these ascetic and anticultural tendencies persisting throughout the history of the church. They are still not dead. We must realize that this anticultural attitude is not biblical. It comes from classical pagan philosophy.

Our attitude to culture as such must not be confused by our attitude to a non- or anti-Christian culture. Christians must acknowledge their task as "salting salt" (Matthew 5:13), not to shun culture, but to try to purify it, or at least preserve it from decay. That is, if we can and if we are allowed to do so by God and by the world around us.

We are children of our age. Whatever culture or age we live in, we are influenced by its ways of thinking, its language, manners, and patterns of life. Therefore, we have no excuse for feeling superior to the early Christians. We should remember the words of Scripture: "Do not be overrighteous, neither be overwise—why destroy yourself? Do not be overwicked, and do not be a fool—why die before your time?" (Ecclesiastes 7:16, 17). We can never analyze everything conclusively—how well Ecclesiastes reminds us of this!—but we should also remember that we ourselves are sinful beings.

Yet we cannot just live as those who surround us. Certainly, so far as we achieve insight into the thoughts and ways of our times, we must beware of accepting them where they are incompatible with Scripture. Failure here prevents Christians from fulfilling their role as a people hungering and thirsting for righteousness, prophets recalling their fellows from the path of disobedience which leads to death—in short, from being salt. Sin manifests itself as greed, lust for power, corruption, misuse of people, racism—and as simple lack of concern. We have to fight these sins in ourselves, but also in the world around us. To be a child of God certainly implies that we can scarcely ever be at ease with the world around us. We may call this attitude the "prophetic pessimism" of the Christian; but it does not entail either accepting things as they are or being perpetually despondent. There is always the hope that sin and its results can be checked or at least mitigated, just as pain can be alleviated even when death is ultimately inevitable.

The Bible contains no criticism of culture as such. Solomon hired people from the pagan world to help build the Temple. Perhaps that could be done in those days. But God's people are always reminded not to follow the pagans' gods or fall into their religious practices. A culture becomes unchristian when the wrong gods are revered and served. Today the gods are pleasure, sex, power, and money: this is the Moloch which Allen Ginsberg denounced with power and accuracy in his poem "Howl." These gods blind us to the true power of sin. The results are becoming plainer every day, as a non-Christian culture reaches maturity and works out the full consequences of its principles: "The earth is defiled by its people; they have disobeyed the laws, violated the statutes and broken the everlasting covenant. Therefore a curse consumes the earth . . ." (Isaiah 24:5, 6; see also Hosea 4). In Ginsberg's own words:

Moloch! Moloch! Robot apartments!
invisible suburbs! skeleton treasuries!

blind capitals! demonic industries!
spectral nations! invincible madhouses! monstrous bombs!
They broke their back lifting Moloch to heaven!
Pavements, trees, radios, tons, lifting the
city to heaven which exists and
is everywhere about us![4]

Indeed the last thought makes clear the difference between the man-made city with its idolatry, and the Kingdom of God.

The biblical symbol of such an evil culture is Babel, where sin and idolatry have come to fruition, although happily never completely so. It is a place of tyrants and impending chaos, a world where the worship of power goes hand in hand with anarchy, where everyone does what seems good in his own eyes and where everybody wants complete fulfillment in this life regardless of what happens to others. The Bible is full of such examples, among others Psalm 73; Isaiah 32:6; 1 Peter 4:1ff.; 2 Peter 2:19. Wealth is Babel's coveted status symbol, bringing power, pleasure, and immediate satisfaction. We also read of Babel, her riches and luxuries, in Revelation 17 and 18. Again, it is not her wealth in itself that is sinful, but the impure passions, the spiritual fornication, the purposes for which the wealth is used—and the dealing in human souls.

So the Bible warns: "Come out of her, my people, so that you will not share in her sins, so that you will not receive any of her plagues" (Revelation 18:4). The catchword is, "Beware! Don't take chances, like Lot whom God had to lead out of the evil city of Sodom. Take no part in her activities, do not bow down before the beast, do not imitate her sinful ways." Here is the real antithesis: not between culture and Christianity, but between the sinful idolatry of this world and loving obedience to God's laws.

"Come out" cannot mean that we should withdraw from this world, letting it go its own way. The Bible calls God's people to care, to help, to be concerned; we are reminded of this in the story of the good Samaritan. Our friendliness must be known to everyone (Philippians 4:5).

Peter's letters teach very clearly how Christians should live in a non-Christian world. "Mere common sense," we may say, and we would be right, but it is biblical common sense! How effectively Peter shows that love is not something simple, and certainly not being soft, sweet, and unprincipled. In 2 Peter 1:5ff. we are told to build knowledge upon virtue. Knowledge here does not mean rationalistic knowledge, but rather wisdom and insight into who man is, and what is right or wrong. Upon knowledge is built self-control, and on that perseverance. Then we come to godliness, leading to brotherly affection, and finally on to love—love for everyone (the kind of love described by Paul in the famous passage, 1 Corinthians 13). Although many things have changed since Peter wrote, the wisdom of these words of God is never outdated, and can still show us how to live in this world.

The prayer of Jesus for his followers was also quite clear in its intentions: "My prayer is not that you take them out of the world but that you protect them from the evil one" (John 17:15). Later he refers again to their way of life, and asks, "May they be brought to complete unity to let the world know that you sent me and have loved them even as you have loved me" (verse 23). To live as Christ prayed should be our most forceful and convincing testimony.

Understanding that the Lord made the world good and that it therefore belongs to him, we should work toward a realization of its concrete potential in the customs we follow, our thought-forms, the lifestyle we adopt, our use of natural resources, our discovery and treatment of beauty. This entails taking action against sin, destruction, corruption, and the lust for power and self-satisfaction. We must forsake Babel, not in order to gloat over her lostness, nor to withdraw our concern for those who still belong to her, but in order to help. We must avoid the pollution of this world not in order to feed our own pride and self-esteem (that would itself be gross pollution, the sin of the pharisees of all times), but to be better able to help, as the salt of the earth.

It is vital that we understand the gospel here. God's gift to us is a Savior who is able to cleanse hearts and forgive sins. Repeatedly in the Bible God urges us to turn back to him and be redeemed from the sins that separate us from him; he wants our relationship with him to be restored and open. Ezekiel 36:25 promises, "I will sprinkle clean water on you, and you will be clean; I will cleanse you from all your impurities and from all your idols." But the text does not stop there, for God says, "I will give you a new heart and put a new spirit in you; I will remove from you your heart of stone and give you a heart of flesh."

We find the same gospel summarized in Colossians 2:11ff. We read again of renewal of the heart, this time in the metaphor of inward circumcision (also found in Jeremiah 4:4). Man becomes a new creature (Romans 6). We read again of forgiveness of sins, and then of the devil's forfeiture of his power. Here then is the gospel: that the power of sin and evil is broken, through the cross.

The importance of this good news goes beyond its offer of salvation for the individual, and even beyond the promise of a new heaven and a new earth. It has immediate relevance for us, because here and now we as a community can be a healing force. Life begins *now* for anyone who has accepted Christ (cf. John 5:24) and for whom death has lost its power; Christ's renewal allows man to live. Though perhaps it may face the danger or even reality of persecution, and will certainly not find ease and total acceptance, the Christian community as a whole has been called to demonstrate that Christ is truly the Savior and renewer. It is only on this basis that we can begin to solve the problem which some call "Christianity and culture," but which we could better describe as "Christianity's place within God's creation."

Even the word "problem" sounds too academic, too intellectual. This is a real life issue, not a problem to be solved in theory at the writing desk. It is the tension in the Christian's life between on the one hand his love for the beauty of God's creation, his fellow-creatures, and his Lord, and on the other hand his battle against sin and death—a tension further complicated by the Christian's knowledge that sin is not only "out there," but also "here" within him.

We must recognize that sin goes much deeper than moral failure. As we have already seen, the Bible points out that following false gods is the real source of the trouble. We read, "The Israelites did evil in the eyes of the LORD; they forgot the Lord their God and served the Baals and the Asherahs" (Judges 3:7). Again and again in Deuteronomy Moses warns the Israelites not to be faithless to the Lord. They were promised cities, vineyards, all the good things of life—we would say "cultural benefits"—but they could enjoy these things rightly only if they did not pollute the land with idols (Deuteronomy 6:10ff.).

This problem of culture can be solved only in Jesus Christ. Not in a rejection of the world—that is more a Greek than a Christian solution. Nor in a following of the cultures around us, with a dash of "Christian religion" thrown in—a God for Sunday and "quiet times." It is a matter of getting our priorities right. Our surrender to God must be without "ifs" and "buts," without restrictions. The other things will follow. God gives his commandments in order that we may live; he is the Creator of life. Jesus said, "If you remain in me and my words remain in you, ask whatever you wish, and it will be given you" (John 15:7).

A colleague of mine once gave a very important lecture, discussing at length the sources and meaning of asceticism. His study, "Culture and Salvation," deals, although in a more specific context, with the issues we have been considering. Here is his conclusion:

> Do we have to say that both are right? Must we say to the ascetic person: God has given the cultural mandate, and if we follow that we are always safe? But the ascetic will answer, rightly, that we have failed to understand the motivation behind culture. What is

the solution? God gives it in the story of creation, and Christ further explains it in his sermon where he tells us not to be afraid and anxious: "Obeying the cultural mandate and accepting culture are right; but first remind yourselves that I am the sense, meaning, and center of culture, and that you can only accept culture if you want my Kingdom, and love me more than yourself." (See Matthew 6:33.) More specifically in Mark 10:28-31 Jesus expands his words "seek first my Kingdom and all these things (food and clothes) shall be added unto you" with the concrete explanation that already now, in this life, those who have faith in him will receive houses and land in his name. But only on one condition: that they first forsake everything for Christ. The tragedy of the ascetic has been that he has left out the words "in this life" or has explained them away. He has failed to understand that Jesus gives us back the things of this world if we have first forsaken them for his sake.

Indeed, provided we have no false gods and are clear about our priorities, we can creatively engage in cultural activity. But in the same text in Mark we also find a warning that there may be persecutions, and that we may have to lose everything, including our lives, just *because* we have set our priorities right. Nevertheless, the promise holds for a great and real future.

As Matthew 7:13, 14 reminds us, there are two ways. One lies through the narrow gate that leads to life, and the other has an open and easy entrance, but leads to destruction. The narrowness of the gate does not mean that the gospel is not open to everybody. The gate is narrow in that when we go through it we must leave behind our pride, our self-reliance, our autonomy. (Many people would prefer to be asked to make difficult sacrifices or be given special assignments because that would make them special people, part of a respected in-group with grounds for pride.) The broad way seems to be open and easy, for it coincides with our deepest longings and strivings; it promises to fulfill our wishes and free us to do as we please. The breadth of this road is deceptive, for it soon takes away our freedom, and leads to destruction and death.

Man's choice at the crossroads is not just a religious one, set apart from the rest of life, in a kind of supernatural "spiritual" realm. It has concrete consequences, a harvest, the "fruits" mentioned in Matthew 7:17, 18, 20. What are these fruits, if not what we in our time call culture: the way we live our lives—our style, our influence, our insights, our convictions, and, flowing from these, our actions?

Finally, it is not our work, but God's, to judge the world, as is clear in the Old Testament, in Revelation, and in the last addresses of our Lord (Matthew 24). Our calling is simply to help our fellow-beings, to love them with deeds rather than with words. Ours is not the dilemma posed by Camus in his book *The Plague*—that if man's ills were sent as a judgment by God, then doctors go against God's will when they relieve human suffering. Camus was right when he showed that the plague had something—a great deal, in fact—to do with God's actions. The priest was right in calling the people to repentance. But the doctor was also right when he tried to alleviate their plight. The Bible tells us that God is acting in history, and that suffering is part of the curse. But judgment is not our work. We are merely to help, and to explain the truth in a prophetic way.

Today the Christian community has a special place in the midst of hardships, when the "four riders" of Revelation 6 are passing over the earth bringing famine, war, and death. We need not fear, for like the Israelites whose houses were sealed with blood on the eve of their departure from Egypt, we too are sealed (Revelation 7). The Lord knows who are his. In the beautiful story in Jeremiah 45, Baruch, the secretary of the prophet, looks with dread into the future; but the Lord has a special message for him: Although judgment is coming, God will protect Baruch.

Meanwhile, we are to "Seek righteousness, seek humility" (Zephaniah 2:3), acting with integrity, obeying God's commands, and not compromising with the ways of the world. There is no room for the pretension that we can change history, or even save ourselves; our involvement in culture must not be with the idea that God needs the assistance of our great accomplishments. Humility implies looking to him for shelter in the day of adversity, as Zephaniah suggests. His words are nearly the same as those of Christ to seek God's Kingdom first, and the rest will come.

Part Two: Freedom Within a Framework

CHAPTER THREE
Creativity in Love and Freedom

As we saw in the last chapter, culture is concerned with economics, social conditions, and everyday life. Yet it is far too often considered something special, rather odd, and impractical—all very well for an elite that has the time and brains for it. In our own time a noticeable split has occurred in which certain activities, including art, have come to stand apart from and outside of economic and social life.

When culture is seen in this way as something special, then creativity becomes something special too. It becomes a hobby for those who are looking for recreation. Here we can sense the influence of romanticism, which regarded art as a kind of religion—deep, yet remote from reality—and the artist as a high and sublime creative being, a high priest of culture.

We have seen that it is important to think directly from a biblical world- and life-view about our work, our creative powers, and our lives as human beings, beginning by acknowledging our need of God. We shall now specifically consider creativity, how with our own personalities and God-given freedom we can help to shape reality, and how this leads to culture.

In doing this, Christians are not doing something special or peculiar. The non-Christian also feels free to talk about his work as a human being living within a cultural framework—or perhaps moving towards a new framework. He does this from his own world-view. Why should a Christian not do the same? We need not feel apologetic in the face of approaches which call themselves scientific or scholarly, for our starting point is the full reality of the world, made by a Creator who has revealed himself in human language, in Scripture.

CHRIST THE CREATOR: MAN IN HIS IMAGE

John 1 and Hebrews 1 affirm that the world was created through the Word, meaning Christ, and that nothing can exist without him, for he is the foundation of all that is. As the Creator, in whose image all men are made, Christ is therefore also the source of man's creative powers.

Furthermore, Christ's Lordship over creation is also the model for man's relationship to it—a relationship of love and freedom. Man was unique, the crown of God's creation, with all created things at his disposal. The uniqueness of his relationship to both God and the world is at once apparent in the name-giving with which man started his activities (Genesis 2), for giving a name is more than just labeling things in an arbitrary way. It means ordering, finding relationships, and perceiving individual qualities. It means discovering, not inventing (for man does not really invent anything), what the created world in its inexhaustible multiformity and variety has to offer.

God's Framework for Man's Creativity

One cannot, however, make such discoveries without respecting the given realities of the world. No human activity can take place outside the appropriate structural laws, whose presence in creation provide man with a norm for all his undertakings. Language and expression, thinking, administering justice, acquiring knowledge, making or recognizing something beautiful—all are possible only within structural laws. We cannot live and work outside them. They give meaning to all our activities, whether we are simply feeding animals or boiling water. Even someone who wants to commit suicide has to take these laws into account, or his attempt will fail.

We should not see these laws as a deterministic system which compels us to do certain things. That is why I prefer the term "norm" to describe them. Because they are founded in Christ and determine the reality in which we live, we as creatures can work well only if we act according to them. Nevertheless, our relation to them is not one of compulsion, but rather of love and freedom.

Freedom and love are inherent in being human, part of our essential nature. They are at one and the same time a gift, and a guideline to enable us to live effectively. God "commands" us to love and to be free (Galatians 5:1); and although the word "command" for many connotes restriction, God's words are not meant to be a prison, but just the opposite. Man was not created for the law, but the law for man (see Christ's words on the law of the Sabbath in Mark 2:27).

The command to love provides the true basis for freedom. To love our neighbor involves allowing him his rightful freedom as a human being, and at the same time using our freedom in ways that are good for him. To love creation includes thankful use of its potential, ruling over it as lords rather than as tyrants.

The structural laws which constitute the world in which we live cannot be dissociated from our relationship to God. God gave man everything, including life with all its potential, and said, "It is good" (Genesis 1). Because the whole structure of reality is based on Christ (cf. Colossians 1:15-19; Ephesians 2:20-22), man cannot live outside of Christ without ruining life and bringing about destruction.

The Fall: God's Framework Distorted

The Fall meant, essentially, that man wanted to be like God, to determine his own course of action. Man, ceasing to love God, also refused to accept all we have as his gift. Instead of a lord of creation, man became a tyrant over reality—creation reduced to mere "reality," a tremendous impoverishment. His view of things thus reduced, man tried to manipulate them, violating their very nature. And as we see very soon after the Fall, his failure to force animals and human beings to do what went against their nature drove him to cruelty, slavery, and even murder. The man who wants to rule in tyranny finds that reality itself resists him and frustrates his activities. Then not only is love dead, but freedom is lost as well.

Fallen man refuses to see that reality is founded in Christ. Isolated from their true Source, things and actions become merely accidental, part of an attractive and entertaining game, but having no positive end or purpose. Instead of a wonderful totality, displaying unity in diversity, reality loses its touch with truth and becomes a mass of unrelated facts. Perceiving phenomena as things in themselves totally unrelated to Christ, man futilely tries to distinguish order and meaning. He may even conclude that whatever order he discerns is of his own making, a result of his attempt to escape chaos. "What is the meaning of meaning?" asks modern philosophy, paradoxically forced to think about meaning upon realizing its absence.

Man, however, cannot live with the full consequences of this situation. Though he may claim that nothing is worth fighting or dying for, if someone he loves is hurt, his emotions are inconsistent with his philosophy, and he reacts with indignation or sorrow. People who refuse to recognize God nevertheless continue to seek a foundation and meaning for things, even if their starting point provides them no basis for doing so. This tension causes the lives of thousands to remain empty, superficial, and unpredictable; what they accept one day, they reject the next. Without a foundation, even acts of goodness have something accidental and arbitrary about them.

When man abandons the root or core of reality not only theoretically, but in his understanding and experience of life, then he loses his connections, his relation to things. The result, spoken of in modern philosophy, expressed so strongly in modern art, is alienation: life in an absurd world, surreal, among strangers. Even the reality of other people may become oppressive, for they limit me. The world is a strange prison with no exit, no way of escape, as described in Jean Paul Sartre's famous play. Reality is bizarre, irrational, incomprehensible.

Once things exist independently like this, alien both to us and to each other, they are accompanied by death. Paul asserts in 2 Corinthians 3:6 that "the letter [of the law] kills"; apart from God and his love, the law (including the structural laws mentioned above) only shows our weakness, our shortcomings, our helplessness. It shows that we are lost.

Separated from the Lawgiver, law becomes a deadly tyrant. The norm, the law intended to lead to life, can, when man gives it a concrete form, become a harsh demand, whereby man in the end is dehumanized into a thing "under the law." He becomes a slave of the very systems he has constructed (often with the best intentions) to make everything go smoothly and be of maximum usefulness to him. We see this concretely in our own culture since the Enlightenment, where man is reduced to a "cog in the machine"; we also see it in current dictatorial political systems, which devaluate men to an instrument of the State.

Apart from Christ, the norm becomes a source of frustration, a hindrance. This happens when the relationship with a personal God has been replaced by idolatry; a man who does not recognize a transcendent Creator has to choose in God's place something immanent, something belonging to the created order. Everything then becomes related to this god and, since man cannot change the real structure of the creation, everything is distorted. This god may be nature or some other natural force (naturalism); reason (rationalism); morals (moralism); fertility (either the old worship of Venus or Astarte, or the modern worship of sexuality); and so on.

Finding himself caught in a demanding ideal of his own making, man again tries to break away to recover his humanity and his freedom by dissociating himself from the norm, the structure which he formulated for himself. The inevitable result is lawlessness. The composer John Cage "wrote" a piece of music, "Four Minutes Thirteen Seconds," which consists of total silence for that duration of time—"silence which may then be filled up by the sounds of the world itself." Yves Klein did paintings which are just uniformly blue, leaving the beholder completely free to give them his own meaning. Certainly freedom is won in this way, but it is a meaningless and essentially inhuman freedom since there is no possibility of communication. As such, it means death and absolute alienation; it is a possibility only if we say with John Cage: "Here we are. Let us say yes to our presence together in Chaos."[1]

CHRIST THE REDEEMER: RESTORED PURPOSE

From this state of misery, described in the Bible and observable in human experience, Christ can redeem man. He can liberate him from death and alienation and sin. Being redeemed in Christ is not just a subjective experience, a "leap in the dark." It is described in some profound words from the Old Testament, quoted by Paul in the Epistle to the Romans: "The just shall live by faith." These words have a concrete relevance to our lives. Being "just" means (among other things) being in a right relationship to the structural laws of our reality. "Faith" means being founded in Christ and directed towards God. "Live" means standing in freedom, openness, love, responding to the norm with understanding, rather than bent under the law in an enforced obedience.

Life

All men are concerned with life; and God himself wants to

be known as the "God of the living." Life, however, is something much greater than the biological phenomenon studied by the scientists, although of course life includes this. Life is more than the heartbeat, more than being able to move about and observe things. Conversely, we can understand something of what life means if we think of the expression, "to lead a dog's life." A man may be biologically alive, but his existence totally joyless. Never was this better expressed than when a young hippy asked, "Is there a life before death?" This is typical of the conflict facing modern man: he wants to live, but he has rejected the foundation of life. He longs for life and tries to reach out for it in adventure, in sex (called "free love"), in lawlessness, but all he finds is death. This is the tragedy of our times. One would have expected that autonomous man would extol his life without God as something beautiful and good. Sometimes he does try to find something positive and optimistic, but reality forces him to admit his misery and alienation. Martin Esslin says at the end of his book *The Theatre of the Absurd:* "The dignity of man lies in his ability to face reality in all its senselessness."[2]

Life before death can begin only with the new birth in Christ. Only he can restore man to a meaningful relationship with reality. He gives man the power and the desire to do what is right, to act in love and freedom.

Love

Love stands alongside those other basic realities which are the essence of human existence—life, truth, righteousness, freedom, and beauty. The one is not possible without the other. To define love is difficult if not impossible, for it affects us too closely to be summed up in a few words or sentences. Nevertheless, as human beings we do recognize, experience, and in a measure understand love.

Usually we notice love only in very intensive forms, like the growth of passion between a man and a woman, a response of delight to something beautiful in the world, or the wonder of a new convert when he discovers what God has done for him. We often fail to realize love's full significance until we are without it, and life has become cold and ugly.

Paul has given us some penetrating observations on the absence of love in 1 Corinthians 13: if there is no love, then all wisdom, righteousness, purity, truth amount to nothing. They become noise, idle sound, devoid of meaning. Paul wrote these words as a warning to Christians who would give the impression that as long as doctrine is sound, everything is all right. Here is where so many church people fail; they seem to fear love as a mark of weakness.

When this happens, it shows how little they have understood the nature of love. For if their love has not expressed itself in the form of gentleness, patience, regard for others, meekness, and perseverance (the marks of Christian love according to 1 Corinthians 13:4-6; Galatians 5:22; and 2 Peter 1:5-7), then all their righteousness is empty, their exertion for the church fruitless, and their purity of doctrine useless. The Kingdom of God can never be built in this way.

The Four Freedoms

Freedom without love would be licentiousness, but love without freedom is not really love. Together they determine what it is to be human. Again and again in his epistles Paul explains the basis of real freedom. In Colossians 2:11-15 Paul shows first that man's life is renewed in Christ; he refers to Jeremiah 4:4, which speaks of circumcision of the heart. Then he declares that men's sins are forgiven (vs. 13). Finally, he mentions the defeat of the devil (vs. 15).

Paul continues with a magnificent passage on Christian freedom. Christians who make rules for other Christians to obey, or who accept such rules, show how little they understand the renewed life offered in Christ. They are worldly, says Paul (Colossians 2:20). One might even say they are secularizing the Christian life. As the apostle says elsewhere: "You did not receive a spirit that makes you a slave again to fear, but you received the Spirit of sonship. And by him we cry, 'Abba, Father' " (Romans 8:15).

Freedom is a fruit of the Spirit. It means that we are *free before God.* Like Jesus, we may call him "Father." John speaks of our "confidence before God," which means an open and straightforward relationship, without fear (1 John 3:21). Although our freedom must not be confused with forwardness and impudence, we may stand in love and confidence before a personal God. For no matter how some Christians have unfortunately regarded him, God is not Fate, a bogy, or a sadistic spectator eagerly waiting to punish our every failure. The Bible would have us see him as a beloved Father whom we regard with reverence and awe, and try not to grieve.

If we have founded our lives in Christ and are free before God, we are also *free towards ourselves.* We need not be afraid to be ourselves, for Christ has accepted us as we are, with our own personalities. We are free to develop our own individuality. Frustration and self-mortification do not belong to the gospel, as Paul points out in Colossians 2:16-23. Yet self-realization is also not the aim of the man made new in Christ; for him, life is both a gift and a task addressed to him as an individual.

Freedom towards the world is another privilege of the Christian. Christians may suffer in the world, because the world also made Christ suffer (1 Peter 4:12-16); but Jesus said we should not be afraid of the world, which may kill the body but cannot kill the soul (Matthew 10:28). We need never seek an undesirable compromise; we have true freedom because we are in God's hands. He has counted the hairs on our heads and knows our needs (Matthew 6:25-34). As his servants, we can perform our duty, but we need not worry as if the fate of the world depended on our actions. This trust in God liberates us from the need to calculate and determine everything ourselves.

Because God wants to work through our weakness (see 1 Corinthians 2:1-5, and the verses preceding), and has pledged himself to answer our prayers liberally, as his children we are free to work without pressure, without fear, without superiority or inferiority complexes. We are not alone, and we do not depend on our good works to gain us a place in Heaven.

The *Heidelberg Catechism* makes the same point in regard to the church. "From . . . beginning to . . . end . . . the Son of God gathers, protects and preserves" the church.[3] It is not our responsibility. Responsibility for the church would be too heavy a burden for its leaders, who would feel a need for rules, ecclesiastical police, and spiritual tyranny.

Only God can give man the freedom we are describing, and enable his children to live together in this freedom. He maintains and protects them—and even adds to their number. Christians may preach the gospel, but it is God who calls men to himself. God's children may admonish and support each other, but it is God who maintains his church. It is disastrous when those who think they know better try to maintain the church themselves, like the minister who wrote to his friend, "Things are going well here; the church is getting purer, even though fewer and fewer people come to the services." One remembers the figure of the Grand Inquisitor in Dostoyevsky's *The Brothers Karamazov:* the church leaders had corrected the mistakes of Christ, who was too idealistic! In all ages this way of thinking has perverted the church—Roman Catholic, Eastern Orthodox, and Protestant churches alike.

How much religious strife would have been avoided if Christians had understood that it is their task to be kind, patient, gentle, humble, regarding others better than themselves. Although church people may have their responsibilities, all final judgment is reserved for God (Romans 12:19).

Finally, freedom in Christ gives man *openness towards nature.* God's creation lies open before us; and because he is Lord, we need not fear it as a malevolent force. It is also not a system that runs by itself, explainable in terms of a mechanical law of cause and effect. Such laws may describe how the world functions, but they stop short of touching its deepest reality: the world is open, and God is active in it (cf. Deuteronomy 27—30). That is why it has meaning to pray for blessings, to give thanks before eating, or to have a national Thanksgiving Day.

By contrast, the mechanistic universe of modern science is indeed something to be feared, for it functions as an entity completely unrelated to man's actions or will. Admittedly we do not understand everything in nature, and cannot provide a theological rationale for every plentiful harvest or natural disaster. But that does not mean that everything happens by chance, by natural laws unrelated to man's situation. Because the world is open, we must take into account the curse and God's judgment.

But even if we here arrive at the limits of our human understanding, if with Job (Job 40:6ff.) we stand awe-stricken at God's wisdom in nature, we need not see nature as a prison that frustrates our plans and activities; this occurs only when we make demands upon it that go against its created order, those structural norms we have already mentioned.

So we can be free towards nature, since as God's creation it is the environment he gave us to inhabit. We are at home here. Alienation is unnecessary. Contact with reality at a deep level is part of the Christian's life. He enters into reality rather than escaping from it. The flight from reality is a mark of Eastern and classical mysticism, not of Christianity.

Of course, our freedom is limited by the curse (Romans 8:18ff.) and also by sin. Because of the Fall, nature is not fully as God intended, and we must put restraints upon it. Nature's occasional hostility and recalcitrance show that the curse is real. But the curse does not have the last word, for in Christ there is the promise of ultimate renewal, and even now our relationship with nature can be marked by renewal and restoration.

This may all sound rather obvious. Yet anyone who has understood even a little of what is involved in the pursuit of autonomous freedom—with its alienation, frustration, and the sense of imprisonment in one's own existence—will understand that such freedom and openness are anything but a matter of course. (See Chapter 5, on Buñuel.) Nor are such freedom and openness cheap; Christ had to die to give them to us. Outside him, the love and freedom of ordinary humanity are lost.

The Christian's Battleground

Christ's coming into the world has brought back the possibility of life, love and freedom, but these are not to be had without a struggle. The Christian must wage war on two important fronts, the first of which is within himself. Sin is in our bones; it tries to drive us back to self-determination, self-protection, self-reliance. It tries to draw us away from God and tempts us not to use his gifts, nor to believe the promise that he will answer our prayers.

But sin is also outside us, in the world, where the effects of the Fall are still a hard reality. Christians therefore must fight against the misery and imperfection around them—injustice, falsehood, corruption—things that take away man's freedom and put him in a cage of fear, frustration, and guilt.

TRUE HUMANNESS IN CHRIST

The new life in Christ is all-inclusive. It means living creatively with God's help, through prayer. In Christ, God gives us the opportunity of living; it remains for us to build on this possibility, this foundation, with the talents we have been given—whether to sing, to paint, to build, or to manage a home. But in order to erect a building that is more than hay or stubble, we must let Christ produce the fruit of the Spirit in our lives. That is what it means to be truly human.

Creativity in Everyday Life

Creativity, then, is what we make of our own lives. Each life is an individual possession, but each life also touches the lives of others, in community. Christians speak here of the "communion of saints." At every point we are involved with others, working in and for the world to renew and maintain it, to set things right, to restore peace. We are to do this not primarily on a large scale, but in a small way among the people around us, which is the most difficult thing of all!

This is what it is to serve the truth, in love. Truth is not a concept to be formulated and defended; it is something to be *done* (John 3:21). Doctrine that is sound must express itself in godlike behavior, for God considers mere lip-service abominable (Isaiah 29:13). He wants to involve us in restoring relationships and situations. We will have to work and think, seizing the opportunity to benefit other people within the realm of everyday experience.

Often this sort of work is anonymous; the people connected with it may know of the effort involved, and one may perhaps receive some public honor, but even then the work (making laws or roads, building houses or organizations, even producing works of art) is ultimately unacknowledged and meant for the benefit of mankind. Whether our work will last or will continue to be honored is unimportant. At this point, the wisdom of Ecclesiastes runs directly counter to all human striving to make an eternal reputation.

Such work will always be in conflict with evil and the Evil One. By fighting against the incompleteness of the world, by renewing and improving it, we are taking part in the very real struggle against evil and destructive spiritual powers.

Creativity in the Narrow Sense

Besides the more general matters mentioned above, there is a more limited kind of creativity which leads to a particular creation like an invention or a work of art. Between the kind of creativity discussed above and the latter, for which the term is usually reserved, is no material difference.

Looking in the Bible for an example of the narrower kind of creativity, we find Bezalel and Oholiab who are mentioned in Exodus 31. Bezalel is described as being "filled with the Spirit of God, with skill, ability and knowledge in all kinds of crafts" (verse 3). Oholiab has the skill to carry out the designs of Bezalel. Since Bezalel makes designs, he is a shaper of culture *par excellence.* He is a man who discovers new possibilities; he opens up creation and cultivates it, and he does so with wisdom and understanding. Wisdom is the capacity to see relationships, understand what is and is not possible or meaningful, what contributes to humanity, dignity, righteousness, purity, harmony—in short, everything which serves life in a positive way (Philippians 4:8).

Inspiration

Creativity in any specific sense does not come of itself. Inspiration is necessary. Nowadays, the old conception of inspiration as a spiritual influence from outside man has completely vanished. Even if the word is occasionally used, its real sense is denied. It tends to be employed to indicate a certain physical condition during the act of creation, when everything goes well for instance, and the artist is able to concentrate. But the idea that there might be any influence on man from outside is not considered at all.

Without inspiration, creativity becomes a continual search to find something new, without any concern to make a real contribution to humanity and the conditions of life in this world. In his creativity, man may be inspired by the Holy Spirit as in the case of Bezalel; indeed, God's Spirit is needed to produce what is truly beautiful or positive. Yet God can also give the Spirit to nonbelievers, to inspire them in their creativity. This gift never comes automatically, although to the nonbeliever it comes unsought. It comes because God thinks a certain thing necessary for his creation, for the benefit of men, women, children, and animals (see Jonah 4:11). The latter may not belong to his people in the more limited sense, but they do belong to his creation.

When speaking about creativity, we need not think only of the work of the artist. We can also include the work of inventors. Surprisingly often these men describe how a long-sought solution has flashed upon them from outside, through inspiration, in a sudden moment of clarity. There is evidence of remarkable guidance in their research. R. E. D. Clark gives some striking examples in *Christian Belief and Science.* He quotes men like Helmholz, Faraday, and Gauss, the latter asserting that although it was he himself who achieved certain results, he cannot explain how.[4]

Much creativity also occurs without the guidance of the Spirit, especially in this day when man prefers to be emancipated from God. He wants to do things himself and regards the consideration of forces and powers outside human subjectivity as antiquated superstition. But without God, without Christ, without the Spirit, our work lacks purpose. It becomes neutral and cold. This can be seen in Darwin's autobiography, wherein he describes how as a young man he used to love poetry and music, but that he can bear them no longer. Even the appreciation of natural beauty is almost entirely lost for him. "My mind seems to have become a kind of machine for grinding general laws out of large collections of fact."[5] He notes that the loss of his taste for art has affected his happiness and certainly weakened his emotional life.

Without the influence of God's Spirit, man has to rely on his own subjectivity to provide the creative force. Often he tries to achieve this by transgressing all intellectual and moral boundaries, giving free rein to his passions, perhaps using drink or drugs to stimulate his subjectivity. This results in creations which would not otherwise have come into being. It cannot be proved that a clear mind and judgment would have led to something more profound and lasting, but such a conclusion seems obvious. We can also trace the preference for improvisation and spontaneity, for all that is unstudied and unreasoned, to this modern predilection.

Lastly, we may mention the possibility of inspiration by diabolical forces. There are truly devilish crimes, which are sometimes even committed out of a kind of delight in the perverse. Literature gives us examples like the character of des Esseintes from Huysman's *A Rebours,* written in 1884, and the strange inspiration which led de Sade to conceive and write *Justine* (1791). The character of Faust may be similarly understood.

In real life, such phenomena occur more frequently than is often realized. One must be prepared to recognize that the "spiritual forces of evil in the heavenly realms" (Ephesians 6:12) do indeed exert an influence on the lives of human beings. (The more one considers these matters, the more one realizes how much even Bible-believing Christians have been brainwashed by contemporary patterns of thought which deny the existence of objective spiritual forces. How great is the consequent impoverishment of their understanding.)

In view of all this, we can see the importance of praying, "Deliver us from evil." The fact that our Western world is still relatively free from evil forces like black magic and occult occurrences may be the result of this prayer. If people today think this unimportant, the reason may be that people in previous ages did pray this prayer with understanding. For the Germanic tribes who became Christians between A.D. 500 and 1000, this deliverance from the devil and from evil forces, often equated with the old gods, was the center of Christ's work. This can be seen if one carefully studies early Romanesque art.

Artistic Freedom

Even granted the presence of inspiration, there is no creativity without freedom. If a person always has to ask himself, "What will people think?" or "Have I taken this or that into account?" he will achieve nothing, for he will be relying on laws and rules made by others rather than those belonging intrinsically to the thing he is creating, the content already present in God's creation. The man who would be creative must be free from legalistic thinking; how, for example, could anyone compose songs in a milieu where all but sacred hymns were considered evil?

Whoever would create must be free from the past, the

present, and the future. He cannot do things just for the sake of tradition, although he may work within traditions and even uphold them. He need also not be a slave of current fashion, although he may appreciate its contributions. Nor should he be concerned only with the future significance of his work, stifled in his creativity by a vain search for glory.

Although a work of art comes into existence in a contemporary situation, and is perhaps made for a certain purpose, it must not be forced into an imposed framework. The artist must be free to realize the commission in his own way, his own style. A person who gives a commission may ask for a piece of music of a certain length, for a book on a certain subject, or for a wall decoration of a certain size. These are requirements belonging strictly to the commission, and may challenge the artist to find the right solutions. They do not as such take away his freedom, but rather give him a chance to do something meaningful, something with a function. However, an artist must never be asked to comply with norms which he finds altogether alien and which are outside the scope of a given commission, as for example, "A Christian novel must always have a happy ending" or "A Christian should write only sacred poetry." If the group to which an artist or any creative person belongs is censorious, either his talent will be stifled or he will be forced to leave his own milieu.

There must also be freedom in a person's use of material necessary to accomplish the creation. Within the limits of the task assigned, a free use of materials may lead to development of new materials and new methods.

Basically, one should be free to do what is right. Christian freedom is not freedom *from* something, but *to do* something. It means openness, freedom of movement, exploration, and mental adventure.

Responsibility

The freedom we have been describing can never exist apart from love. We never create in a merely individualistic way, in a vacuum. Love means that we have a responsibility, as God's servants, to direct our creativity for the benefit of others. If we ourselves fail to remember our obligation of love, other people may have to curtail our freedom by appealing to our sense of responsibility. This is certainly much more than a mere theoretical possibility within the (orthodox) Christian world. Freedom never means sinful licentiousness or a stubborn individualism that makes us indifferent to the effects we have on others.

Creativity Is Nothing Special

As we have already pointed out earlier in this chapter, when we speak about creativity, we do not mean only art. Creativity is part of everyone's work, wherever the best solution to a task is sought in love and freedom. This applies both to our contribution to social relationships and to our specific work in engineering, in science, in theology—wherever things have to be made or problems solved.

What do we mean when we talk about Western civilization? Is it not what we, Western people, have created? Creativity means growing bulbs, designing a new car, building a computer, discovering certain relationships within molecules, or writing a sermon; all these activites and a thousand more, like town planning, architecture, road construction, but also office work and cooking.

All of these can be done in a creative way. Of course, we must understand that all these activities have their economic and social aspects, and each of them has its place, function, and significance within a larger context. Once the component parts of each aspect are harmoniously related to each other, providing also that the relations between the various aspects themselves are harmonious, then everything is in its proper place. But if, as happens in twentieth-century culture, strong contrasts have developed between on the one hand "culture" in the narrow sense of the word, and on the other hand science and technology, then the result is a disharmony which afflicts us all and which constitutes the crisis of our civilization.

There should be no dichotomy between anonymous works and the creations of individuals, between "industrial design" and what has become autonomous art. This dichotomy stems from the disharmony just mentioned, and is in many ways the consequence of a strongly humanistic view of life.

Christians, having been renewed in Christ, can help to restore the unity of our civilization. They are called to be creative—in their daily lives, in Christian organizations, in their jobs and the fulfillment of their calling. Although some of their activities may look insignificant in the eyes of the world, the historian, or the snob, they may prove very important for human society as a whole and even for the Kingdom of God.

Christian culture is not something special or sacred with a kind of halo around it. On the contrary, it means nothing more, and nothing less, than the building of a civilization within the structures, laws and norms given by God. In the end it is all very commonplace and ordinary—what could be more ordinary than the healthy and the good? But as history and experience tell us, these are precisely the most difficult things to achieve in a cursed world populated by a sinful race.

The way is so simple and yet so difficult—so difficult that Christ had to die so that some of it could be achieved now. When as Christians we bring forth the fruits of the Spirit in our lives, we can begin to influence the spirit of human social institutions. Our work may help to form customs and traditions in a positive way, and renewal instead of legalism may help to heal relationships.

These things will come about only if the Lord blesses our efforts and gives us a place of influence (Deuteronomy 28:13). This is not a mechanical process; we could better describe it in organic terms, as the Bible does. A rich general culture, alive and many-sided, can result as a fruit of the fruit of the Spirit (Isaiah 32:15ff.)—a secondary fruit if you like, but nevertheless an important sign of the vitality of Christ's finished work.

CHAPTER FOUR

Authority and Permissiveness

WHAT HAS HAPPENED TO AUTHORITY?

In the last chapter we talked of the freedom of the Christian to live and create. But, as we shall see, this freedom is much different from what most of our contemporaries mean by freedom.

The world we live in is rapidly changing. The structures of society have been radically criticized, and many things rejected. The demand is for a new society, characterized by permissiveness, which is what most people mean by the word "freedom" today.

The relative speed of all these changes has left many people perplexed; they want to know where the sudden landslide of values has come from. And what does it mean?

The Old World-view

Directly linked to this change in modern life—in fact, the very key to it—is an altered world-view, a new attitude to life. During the past three centuries, since the Age of Reason, man's understanding of the world and life has changed out of all recognition. If we go back to a time before this world-view began to change, let us say to the seventeenth century, we find that the people of those days looked at the world as follows:

GOD
The Cosmos

Angels	Men
Devils	Animals
	Plants
	Things

This is also the basic view of the world which we find in the Bible.

Even more important for an understanding of our topic is the fact that this world-view included *norms,* laws which were universally valid. There was a difference between good and evil. There was *order,* there were structures, there were absolute values. And because these structures existed, there was also authority, an authority that was universally accepted. This authority was based on a norm that was just as applicable to the man in authority as it was for the person who obeyed him. This meant that the person in authority did not get his power as a result of his own personal qualities; every ruler, whether he liked it or not, exercised his rule by the grace of God. The whole of society was based on what Paul said in Romans 13 about obedience to the government, for "there is no authority except that which God has established."

People at that time also recognized the existence of sin. They knew that they could not reach perfection in this life, and because of this—and because of the Christian's duty to love his neighbor—they had a certain forbearance for those in authority, recognizing that leaders, too, could make mistakes.

However, a new attitude began to appear in various humanistic circles, an attitude that became more noticeable as the seventeenth century progressed. In the next century, this new philosophy materialized as the Enlightenment.

The Enlightenment–a New World-view

With the Enlightenment, the old world-view disappeared.

The God who had been recognized at the summit of all things disappeared. Whether he—whose name had been totally emptied of meaning by the deists—really existed or not was of no importance. One no longer had any need of him. God was removed from the world, and with him went the angels and the devils as well. With him also vanished the norms which he had established, and which had potency and validity only because of his existence. Finally, along with the norms, the absolute distinction between good and evil faded away, for one could no longer be certain that such a distinction existed.

Thus we have arrived at the world-view which our modern age also accepts as the true one. The whole supernatural portion, the "unseen world" of the old framework, has been removed. All that is left is man and the nature which surrounds him.

A New View of Man

Man since the Enlightenment has become autonomous. No one has authority over him; he is free. But there is more to be said. He is free at a price. The fixed norms have gone. Where is he to find certainties and security? Only the subjective is left. How can he know when something is true? What, if any, is the standard? Mankind, lonely and isolated, must try in its own strength to solve the problems of existence, to find meaning in a life where things have lost their structure.

In the old encyclopedias all information used to be classified, arranged under "animal kingdom," "plant kingdom," etc. But now that God has disappeared from our world-view, nothing has its fixed place any more. In the famous *Encyclopedia of the Enlightenment,* edited by Diderot, we find everything for the first time arranged in alphabetical order. The connecting link has gone. Is man more than an animal? That is difficult to say; man has more understanding, but does that make him more significant?

A process of atomization has taken place, whereby things

now exist independently of each other. The hierarchy of man and animals, things and ideas has been lost forever.

This change has also had repercussions in art. When the Spanish artist Goya depicts the rebellion of his countrymen against the French regime in 1808, the theme is no longer the struggle for freedom, freedom fighters on one side and oppressors on the other. No; men are killing men—that is all that can be said.

WHO SOLVES THE PROBLEMS IN A NORMLESS SOCIETY?

When all norms break down, one of the first effects is in the administration of justice—how can it still be done? Above all, how can one exercise authority? From whom does one really derive his power?

The first philosopher to take on this problem was the Englishman Hobbes, who lived in the seventeenth century. In his book *Leviathan*, published in 1665, he describes the State as a monster. A still more influential figure was Jean Jacques Rousseau who wrote about a century later but who, unlike Hobbes, was optimistic about the possibilities for man without God in this life.

"The Social Contract"

Rousseau declared that man is autonomous, completely free. But because a society made up of strictly autonomous people would rapidly lead to chaos, this new society also needs norms. What can be the base for these norms? Rousseau's answer was the "social contract." According to him, sovereign man in early times gave up his rights to an authority, to the government. This means that all governments are republican in origin. Having first drawn up the laws, the people willingly subjected themselves to these same laws. The authority of the State is thus derived from the authority of each individual. The next step is for the interests of the State to become the norm. This means that, following in the footsteps of Rousseau, we repeatedly come up against an unsolvable dilemma: issuing from the autonomous freedom of man is either chaos—in which case freedom loses its meaning—or dictatorship, whereby man essentially loses his freedom, no matter how one may disguise it all in beautiful words.

We see that there simply is no real norm. A norm can be a norm only if its authority is greater than that of individual men. A true norm must be one which exists outside of man, and which issues from something greater than himself. All agreements on the basis of what is rational (i.e., what we can understand with our reason and accept as being just) are by necessity relative. Our opinions change, our agreements vary, and the structure of society changes as well.

If there are no norms left, then one can obviously no longer use words like "sin." The social sciences have reduced evil and sin to environmental or social structures. Evil surely cannot be metaphysical, can it? The structures will have to be changed. But who is to do this? That is obviously the duty of the State. The State has to come up with the answers. She must attend to economics and general prosperity. She must encourage and promote the well-being of the citizens.

A World Without Fathers

The State is still with us. But where is authority? *There Are No Fathers in the World* is the name of a book by Hans Müllerschäfe, in which he discusses how the world has lost a legitimate hierarchy of authorities. Family ties are broken, people are cut off from one another, everyone works as an individual. Life is atomized. The family no longer has a real father, there are hardly any true teachers and educators left, and last of all there are no true statesmen anymore. We have plenty of experts in the social-economic field—we have experts in this and experts in that—there is no shortage of technicians. But there are no more great leaders.

Our society today no longer has any concept of *office*. An

office is directly related to the fact that we are made in the image of God—prophets, priests, and kings; an officeholder is something more in his official function than he is as an individual. He has authority not because he does something particularly well himself, nor because he is infallible. No; he is in a position of authority because he has been placed there. The norms which he applies, and which also apply to himself, are not meant to give the impression that he himself holds all the laws, but that they originate from an authority higher than himself. And the justice that he dispenses derives its validity ultimately from the judgment of God which is to come.

Without such an "office," every person in authority must justify his own position. His authority can never be rationally proved. Who gives him the right to occupy a particular position of control? Is he competent? Is authority only a matter of the personal prestige of the man in authority, or is it decided by factors other than individual ability? If personal qualities are the only criteria for leadership, then a leader has no real right to prohibit anything, for that would make him guilty of pure paternalism.

Love Grown Cold

Our life, then, has become atomized. This also explains the growing crime rate, the violence and murder which are a direct consequence of a waning respect for the law. The boundaries between society and the underworld have become blurred, a process that has been accelerated by the presence of the "Underground," the subject of so much modern literature. Loss of norms also leads to an increasing hardness of life. Officials today are allowed to make no mistakes; if they do, they are lashed by a storm of criticism or a hate campaign.

Through the mass media we are increasingly confronted with evil. And kindness has gone. Where is the love that overcomes evil? Matthew 24:12 says, "Because of the increase of wickedness, the love of most will grow cold." This is the order in which it is written, and this is the order in which we see it happening in our society.

THE AGE OF PERMISSIVENESS

The idea of permissiveness consists in the freedom of each person to lead his own life. Where that may and does lead is summed up in a book by Roscam Abbing, *Real Challenges to Christendom.* After he has described practices in our society which are on the increase, while not so long ago they were not even discussed, let alone carried out, he says, "Irrational and emotional objections will carry less and less weight. Many will rapidly become accustomed to these practices."

To many people, protests against modern practices indeed seem "irrational." If we look at these things "rationally," what after all is wrong with prostitution, homosexuality, pornography, or drugs? Human reason is the final authority, and reason has no standard by which to judge anything and eventually reject it.

No Involvement

Much of what we see happening before our eyes at the moment, the whole drift towards a society where everyone has "come of age" and is able to decide for himself what he will or will not do, we can also find discussed in 2 Timothy 3 and 2 Thessalonians 1. There we find that sexual matters are discussed very emphatically, sometimes much too emphatically, in our opinion. But if we find the first verses of 2 Timothy 3 overdone, we must ask whether we ourselves have not been infected by this spirit of permissiveness. We must not forget that the letters of the New Testament were also directed to men who had "come of age." Time and again it is pointed out that because the Christian is free, he is not bound to all kinds of rules and regulations. The mature Christian is led by the law of love, by a feeling of responsibility for his neighbors.

The refusal to bear responsibility for one's neighbor is also evident in the current businesslike approach to sex. One can make sure that intercourse has no biological consequences, and there need also be no emotional consequences because man is not involved with his full humanness. Some years ago in California the so-called "sex weekends" were organized. During these weekends in the country everything was allowed—with one condition: there was to be no talk about one's private life. At all costs the participants had to prevent a real meeting in which they would really become emotionally involved with the other person.

The writer Wayland Young shows how there is a very close link between sexual customs and religion. He divides societies into two categories: orgiastic and nonorgiastic. In the latter, of which our Christian civilization is (or was) an example, where monogamy is the custom, we find that human personality is strengthened by the love one bears for one's partner. We see a parallel to this in that a personal relationship can also exist with God, a situation in which one can love and be loved.

Essential to an orgiastic society, however, is the orgy which takes place several times a year, orgies in which each person gives himself to a total stranger in a completely impersonal way. Alongside this goes an impersonal religion—everything becomes diffused.

Lost Identity

In the orgy, man loses his identity. It does not matter with whom we have sexual intercourse, for who are we ourselves anyway? Loss of personality by means of the orgy is also the aim for which many drug-users strive, an aim that has apparently been aroused by the greater influence of Eastern mysticism in the Western world. These phenomena are evidence that there exists in our present culture a drift towards an orgiastic society.

Many customs and habits have become emptied of their meaning and force. You can read about this everywhere; there are many examples of "modern living." The restraints which in former times may have made a person refrain from free sexual intercourse today hardly play a role. We have lost sight of God's judgment. Pregnancy can bè prevented with the pill; warnings from the home—"You'll be put out of the house if anything happens"—mean very little today. In many cases, the family structure itself has broken down.

Changing Taboos

Some time ago, *Newsweek* featured an article, "The Permissive Society," in which it stated: "There is a shattering of taboos in language, fashion, and manners. It is part of the larger disintegration of the moral consensus in America." As a result, the citizens of a state distrust their government, and Roman Catholics no longer feel bound to what the Pope and the Curia lay down about birth control, etc. Meanwhile, the family, formerly the place where children were taught certain values, increasingly fails to fulfill its function. It has become instead an arena for the conflict between the generations.

As stated in *Newsweek*, many taboos based on language have also disappeared during recent years. Pornography has ceased to be chiefly bad language, or to be sold only under the counter. Anything can now be bought which would have been forbidden a few years ago. But the function of profane language has also changed. Even the better writers have turned to the use of obscenity, because they need the most powerful language to express the chaos of modern life. Norman Mailer writes about conditions in the United States: "I have indeed used many obscenities in my books. And I must, although I hate it. But such language is the only metaphor that can express the situation which has brought about Vietnam."

The word "pornography" has come to have a broader application than it used to. One finds books with titles like *The Pornography of Evil* and *The Pornography of Power*. Power has become something dirty, and it makes those who wield it dirty.

Of course, there is another side to permissiveness. New taboos have arisen to replace the old—for instance, the taboo about death. (Death must not be discussed; that would not be good manners in our modern society.) Moreover, there are many who precisely because of too much freedom get into difficulties—those who get a neurosis from modern life, or are shipwrecked in some other way.

Realization of this fact has produced, in a kind of vicious circle, a reaction of idealism and utopianism. Again the structures get the blame for all the misery, so the structures must go; long live freedom! But often the philosophy behind this is anarchy, the theory based on the doctrine of autonomous man. But, as we saw in the case of Rousseau, because the problem for the anarchist is how to renew the structures, how to allow man his freedom but still ensure that society functions, one finds in all this striving the seeds of a new dictatorship. We find repeatedly a tension between freedom and chaos on the one hand, and order and dictatorship on the other. And no one knows the real answer.

The Bourgeoisie

A question that is often asked is: Why is all this happening just now? Why, so long after the Enlightenment, is the "cultural revolution" under way just at the present? The answer to this question also must be looked for in the past. The revolution which we now see is really a reaction against the bourgeoisie. The bourgeoisie, which arose just after the Enlightenment, for a large part were convinced by the philosophers that we could do without God in our world-view. Most people after Darwin were also convinced that man had an evolutionary past, and that human reproduction took place in the same way as it did with animals. The bourgeoisie, however, were not prepared to alter their life-style to bring it into agreement with this new vision. They wanted to go on living as if nothing had happened. Instead of an honest treatment of sex, consistent with their evolutionary view of man, came the Victorian morality with its refusal to discuss sexuality. Morals turned into moralism; man must be respectable.

Much of what we now see is a reaction to all of this. People want to live in accordance with the life-view that they have. They refuse to put up with dishonesty any longer.

And why does this have to happen just now? For years philosophers have laid the groundwork. Throughout the twentieth century, artists and writers have preached first anarchy, and later the absurd. Particularly after the Second World War, a very realistic style in art ("naturalism" in literature) began to predominate. The theater, films, and other media have also helped to pave the way. Television has brought relativism into our homes; news reporters present the news without any moral commentary: this is life as it is, these things are going on at the moment. And nothing more. All together, these influences—along with the crises of our century—have brought us to where we are now.

One can also no longer turn to the State to solve the problems of society, for the State has also lost its face, its image. It is involved in the same crisis. How can the State bring any order into society without possessing authority?

THE CHRISTIAN MINORITY

If we deeply feel the extent and the scale of the problems with which our modern society is faced, one question remains: Do we have an answer?

Yes, we do have an answer; we must have an answer where the world does not. Our answer has two aspects, two levels: the personal and the governmental. On the personal level, we must understand that as Christians we are a small minority in this world and can no longer—as previously—decisively influence the rulings of the State. We shall have to accept our pluralistic society as it is. The Apostle Peter tells us how to live as a small minority in a non-, scarcely, or anti-Christian world. In 1 Peter 3:13ff. he clarifies our position in regard to authority, including non-Christian authority. And he says clearly that Christians may have to suffer for righteousness' sake.

On the organizational level, where each of us has his own place, we must simply do what we can: be salting salt. What we are not called upon to do is defend the Establishment as such; in fact, many aspects of it could be attacked, and rightly so. Often there is much humanism in the forms of society which some Christians so earnestly defend.

What we are also not called to do is to cling to all kinds of rules and regulations as ends in themselves. Legalism is not a Christian virtue. Christianity is not a morality; it is not something static, but something vital and dynamic. It means life with Christ, new life, new humanity. As Christians, we must have the mentality of the Beatitudes. We must hunger and thirst for righteousness, and never compromise. Where possible, we must try to exert positive influence in our pluralistic society. *And we must never ask for the fruits of faith where there is no faith.*

It takes wisdom for a Christian to be involved in society in a fruitful way. It will mean doing all he can to resist the reduction of men to numbers. It will mean defending everyone's freedom, for the Christian too may sometimes require the freedom to oppose issues which the majority favors. It will mean joining forces with those concerned about ecology, the energy crisis, or social injustice. It will mean fighting for healed relationships and a responsible use of creation for the benefit of man, who—whether he knows it or not—is made in the image of God.

CHAPTER FIVE

Art and Freedom: Buñuel and the Bible

A MESSAGE OF ABSURDITY

The Horror of Buñuel's Vision

In this chapter, we shall consider a film by Luis Buñuel, an example of how belief in man's unlimited freedom can lead to a vision of life as meaningless, absurd. The value of considering such a film is that it confronts us with questions so deep that all cheap answers become impossible. Also, it helps us to discover what the gospel really means when it tells us that we are free in Christ. It gives us so much more reason to thank God for this freedom, and to be on our guard that it not be taken away from ourselves and our fellow-Christians by anyone, even leading churchmen.

Interest in the absurd is not confined to modern philosophers, nor to poets and writers. Visual artists were first in the field, and even before 1914 there were examples of absurd art. By the late fifties and early sixties the theater of the absurd had become almost a rage, with plays by Pinter and Albee being performed everywhere. In view of all the propaganda involved and the tone of the artistic discussion, it was almost a new religion, modern, non-Christian, sometimes even decidedly anti-Christian. Yet the theater of the absurd has existed for a long time. Alfred Jarry's *Ubu Roi*, one of the first absurd pieces, was written as early as 1896; it has clearly anarchistic tendencies. And in 1928 Luis Buñuel, later to become very famous, made his debut with his short film, considered since to be of major importance, *Un Chien Andaloux (The Dog from Andalusia).*

Men like Sartre and Camus have long contended that this world is absurd. It is, they argue, so full of contradictions that it cannot fulfill the demands which modern man would like to impose upon it. Although man knows he is man, he cannot account for the fact; it must be true, yet it can't be true. Sartre is certainly right when he says that rejecting God renders the world meaningless. He is also right to recognize that this world, God's creation, will not (fortunately!) allow man to organize it according to his own ideas. Remarkably, Sartre's language is very beautiful and grammatical French. Despite his message, the form of his thinking and writing is not absurd.

In the theater, however, the impact of the absurd is not experienced in words alone; both the acting and the production reveal the writer's thoughts. Actors can give direct expression to the absurdity of our world: its contradictions, futility, and self-deception. Again, in a way, they are telling the truth. The remarkable thing is that they truly communicate; the spectator may not understand what he sees or hears, but he is nevertheless overwhelmed by the message.

This "message" is central for Buñuel. He was disturbed by the critics who had discussed *Un Chien Andaloux* exclusively from the viewpoint of artistic form. They had called it "interesting" and "fascinating," a kind of supreme play which they could talk about quite calmly without having their hearts touched. Or rather, they would not admit that they had been touched, for fear that they might not be thought "in." Buñuel denounced these snobbish connoisseurs as "that crowd which has tried to call 'beautiful' and 'poetic' something which is basically nothing but a desperate cry for murder." The film shows a frustrated love which does not really go much deeper than sexual passion. It shows sadism and murder, viewed by spectators who are indifferent, or only curious without really being moved. It shows a world full of death, rottenness, fear, and pain; lacking not only joy, but also any solace or hope of solution; a world which is evil to the very depths of its being. A more detailed description of the film is not possible, for it is a series of apparently disjointed scenes, strange and nightmarish. According to Buñuel, there is no judgment to set right what is wrong.

Citizens of a welfare state, sitting in our comfortable chairs, only too well cared for, we tend to see Buñuel as abnormal—sadistic, or possessed. All too easily we suppress our deep anxiety about the possibility of war, of economic crisis, of personal death. Buñuel *is* in fact possessed, not in the medical sense, but by a faith, an idea, a conviction which in this film is expressed with a crude and dogmatic surrealism. In his more "normal" later films he says it again: the order of this world is rotten through and through; and unless church and State, laws and norms pass away, a better world can never appear and man will never be free to do any good. Buñuel is a real anarchist who believes in terror and revolution and who preaches lawlessness. Yet as a human being, he is extremely gentle and in no way eccentric or mentally unbalanced.

This makes it all the more clear that he confronts us with very deep questions. How does God answer these in Scripture? Here, too, we find misery and suppression, covetousness and hypocrisy, sensuality, sickness and war, and not just in a simplified scheme, whereby only the wicked fare badly. The psalmist, for example, speaks of the prosperity of the godless (Psalm 73) and the misery of those—including believers—beset by injustice and imminent death.

The Wrath of God

The Bible is realistic, perhaps more realistic even than Buñuel and his companions, when it describes the misery of man. I do not mean this in a merely theological sense. The Bible puts it this way: "The earth is defiled by its people; they have disobeyed the laws, violated the statutes, and broken the everlasting covenant. Therefore a curse consumes the earth; its people must bear their guilt" (Isaiah 24:5, 6). Sin always and immediately brings suffering and injustice, heartlessness and mercilessness (Romans 1:28-32). That is why "the grave . . . opens its mouth without limit" and "both low and high [are] humbled, and the eyes of the arrogant brought low" (Isaiah 5:14, 15). Although there are mockers who dare God to hasten his judgment so that they can see it (Malachi 2:17; 2 Peter 3:3, 4), when the anger of the Lord is kindled against all this immorality, the mountains will tremble and the dead bodies will lie in the streets like dung and refuse (Isaiah 5:25). But when God hides himself and lets man for the time being pursue his own course, that is even worse. The God who hides himself is an angry God (Psalm 89:46; Isaiah 57:17). In that situation, sin is momentarily allowed to go unpunished but divine blessing is withheld.

God, the Lord of lords of the Old and New Testaments, displays his wrath against evil because it should not be there. Evil prevents mankind from living a full life in God's creation, and God's love for man makes him hate the sight of evil.

There is a solution, but not in a revolution which, although it might bring a better social or economic order, would still leave man himself corrupt and inclined to evil. The Bible speaks not of revolution, but of redemption. People are called to repentance. "Repent, repent before the judgment is upon us," is the cry of the prophets. Above all, do not try to cover things up, saying, "Let us eat and drink, for tomorrow we die" (Isaiah 22:13). This is cheap, and no solution.

The Bible apparently agrees with Buñuel about the condition of the world, but would reject his solution. The psalmist might address him with the words, "The fool says in his heart, There is no God. They are corrupt, their deeds are vile; there is no one who does good" (Psalm 14:1). So biblically Buñuel is a fool.

How does a man arrive at this point of foolishness? The book of Ecclesiastes appears initially to agree with Buñuel: "This is the evil in everything that happens under the sun: The same destiny overtakes all. The hearts of men, moreover, are full of evil and there is madness in their hearts while they live" (9:3). Nor can we dismiss this as only a matter of appearances. If our experience is not sufficient, then Psalm 44 says it clearly enough. We have no excuse for fighting Buñuel in a cheap way by declaring him a sadist or accusing him of inhumanity.

The Lord himself burned with anger against death at the grave of Lazarus; his anger flared again, against dishonesty and greed, when he drove the money-changers out of the Temple. Jesus warns us that we will face struggles and dangers, and nowhere does he promise a sentimental peace. He is moved with compassion for the multitude—needy, doomed, ignorant. Buñuel also hungers and thirsts for righteousness. But for him there can never be any righteousness in the world; that is the horror of it.

Buñuel does not know about full-grown love, beauty, or real compassion. Perhaps he believes, contrary to his better knowledge and judgment, in the possibility of a new anarchistic order which would bring freedom and righteousness. Or are we still trying to see Buñuel too much as a dogmatic Marxist? He may be in favor of the Communist revolution, but he nowhere depicts the realization of such a society.

More than once Buñuel blasphemes in his films. Perhaps we should remember that he is a Spaniard, who spent much of his life in Mexico in voluntary exile, so that his blasphemy may be more anticlericalism than anything else. His priests seem to become human only when adversity forces them to stop preaching cheap grace and pointing futilely to Heaven. Here too the Lord Jesus would be on Buñuel's side, for he denounced the Pharisees and accused them of unrighteousness, hypocrisy, and even of despising the law.

Anyone who knows the story of the Grand Inquisitor from Dostoyevsky's *The Brothers Karamazov*[1] will understand why Buñuel protests against that sort of Christianity; it only confirms what he says. This particular point is not where our difference with Buñuel lies. Surely it is part of a Christian understanding of life that evil and suffering are realities; Paul uses the present tense when describing how the entire creation is in travail and pain (Romans 8:18, 22).

A Song in the Night

Despite this, the Bible does not in general appear dark and pessimistic, full of black humor, misery, and despair. Nor does it merge sexual desire and the death wish, and still less does it present terror and revolution as positive social action. The Bible never tells us that we are caught in a world where love cannot exist and where nature in all its aspects is hostile to man.

The man who believes the Bible is appalled by pronouncements like that of de Sade, that for him the greatest torture was his inability to offend or hurt nature. Buñuel, who is spiritually related to de Sade, sees reality as black, awful, rotten, without comfort or escape. The hell in which Buñuel immerses us, where men behave like deadly scorpions, is far from the world which the Bible describes.

We cannot sidestep the discussion between the Bible and Buñuel. In talking about art, we cannot stop at form. And the form, however clever and controlled, is fairly straightforward in Buñuel's work. He himself forbids us to flee into pure abstract contemplation of autonomous art forms; his art is loaded with meaning. How, then, does the Bible contradict him?

We need look no further than Genesis 1, where God himself says that the world is good. Nature itself declares God's glory and proclaims his handiwork (Psalm 19). It does this so clearly that Paul in Romans 1 is able to conclude that man has no excuse if he refuses to recognize God. Even the writer of Ecclesiastes can say that we should be thankful to God for the joys of this life and go on doing our work, "because nothing is better for a man under the sun" (Ecclesiastes

8:15). The Kingdom of God, as preached by the Scriptures and the whole of nature, is righteousness, peace and joy (Romans 14:17).

Although evil, sin and judgment are realities, there is room for love and beauty. Although it may seem that the wicked flourish, we should consider their end (Psalm 73:17-20). And if God does send judgment, it is so that people will repent and understand his will (Ezekiel 6:10; Revelation 9:20, 21).

Our task is to love our neighbor as ourselves; not to repay evil for evil, but to think of what is honest, proper and noble in everyone's sight; and to pursue peace (Romans 12:17, 18). We must leave the path open for God's wrath, not taking it into our own hands (Romans 12:19).

Possibly the deepest error and sin of Buñuel and the other anarchists is that they themselves want to eliminate evil, to terrorize it away. They hate their fellow-man, instead of loving him in his weakness and helping him towards the good. To hunger and thirst for righteousness means to promote goodness and justice, not to trample upon our neighbor in hate.

Happiness, beauty, and love belong to man, who is created for them and can enjoy them even today, in the midst of God's curse pronounced upon sin. This is the testimony of countless believers down through the centuries. That is how Rinkart, a minister who had seen and lived through all kinds of misery during the Thirty Years' War and had buried thousands of dead, could create the song which is so well-loved in the German- and English-speaking worlds: *"Nun Danket Alle Gott"* ("Now Thank We All Our God"). That is how Schütz in the midst of that same misery could write such beautiful praises to God, using either the words of Psalms or texts written for his own time. He refers directly to this most horrible war when in 1641 he composes *"Aufer Immensum, Deus Iram"* ("God, Let Thy Terrible Wrath Pass Away from Us"). Nor should we forget that the golden age of Dutch art coincided with a long war. And who could forget the message of the Negro spirituals, whose testimony is especially miraculous because they were sung by slaves, or by those who although perhaps emancipated were still suppressed and miserable? Cannot everything we have said be summarized in a sentence from one of those "gospel songs": "I have lost all I lived for; God bless all I live for"?

Although the Christian knows about the good, the true, and the beautiful, the humanist also speaks about these as ideals. Men of all ages have known joy in great and little things. I have already quoted elsewhere the line from a well-known musical in the thirties: "Without a song, there ain't no love at all."

That sound has not been silenced today; its testimony is still there, in songs, in comedies, in cartoons, even in advertisements which go against the fashion of celebrating the blackness of misery and death—a fashion which recognizes Buñuel as one of its exponents. In spite of existentialism, anarchy, and dread of reality, men in our age have made much that is positive, beautiful and good.

Many beautiful things have also been created in painting, music, and film, either serious or as "mere entertainment." The evidence against Buñuel and his kindred spirits—the creators of "modern art" in its more narrow definition—is enormous. The testimony of the Bible, of believers and many unbelievers, of humanists past and present, is that the whole of creation and all humanity were intended to be beautiful, good and joyous.

In a paradoxical way Buñuel himself also testifies to this. Although his whole work stems from the belief that misery is indeed inescapable, and that this world is irredeemably bad, he does not want to resign himself to the world, and senses the horror of what he has said. He is in rebellion against this world precisely because he cannot accept it as he sees it. Nor can he find a way out of its misery. The strange thing is that one can talk of misery, injustice, or deceit only on the basis of a known and accepted norm which reveals these things for what they are! Buñuel is not a devil who loves evil, but a human who rises in protest with his whole being against what Christians would call sin. In church historical terminology, he is a gnostic, a person who believes that life on this earth as such is contemptible. But he no longer knows how to be redeemed because he has cast God aside; there is no exit and no freedom. Buñuel claims that it was surrealism that taught him to see that man is not free.

So we have arrived at our subject: freedom and art. We have tried to confront Buñuel's vision with the biblical outlook, for the depth of his questions demands no lesser answer than that of God's revelation.

FREEDOM AND ART

Modern Art: Man in a Cage

The reader, who may have concluded that this chapter is about freedom or the lack of freedom, and not about art, should be reminded that in modern art we meet these ideas in many forms. Buñuel is not alone. He is closely allied to the Surrealist movement, and thereby to such prominent artists as Picasso, Miró, Ernst, Dali, Breton, and Joyce. But even those who may not have chosen exactly this style express similar ideas. Sartre does it in *Huis Clos:* "Hell is other people";[2] Henry Miller in *Tropic of Cancer:* "If I am inhuman, it is because my world has slopped over its human bounds, because to be human seems like a poor, sorry, miserable affair, limited by the senses, restricted by moralities and codes, defined by platitudes and isms."[3] And he makes it clear that such a vision has everything to do with art: "Anything that falls short of this frightening spectacle, anything less shuddering, less terrifying, less mad, less intoxicated, less contaminating, is not art. The rest is counterfeit. The rest is human. The rest belongs to life and lifelessness."[4] Do we realize what Miller is saying? What he presents us with is art, no matter how horrible; anything else would be human, would mean life. But it would then be a lie, a fake, a false reality.

To show that we meet this idea not only in modern authors, but also in the visual arts, I would prefer to lead you through the rooms of the art galleries and confront you with Raysse, Rauschenberg, Paolozzi, Couzijn, Guston, Wols, Baj, Saura, Tapies, Dubuffet, Richier, Matta, Lam. . . . We could extend this list without any trouble. Perhaps a quotation will clarify what I mean. Hans Platschek, an intelligent German artist and admirer of Wols, wrote about the latter: "With Wols the proper theme is . . . the possibility of catching images even when not only the protocol of art, but also the protocol of reality is denied by it." That is why "to him the art of painting is the embodiment of doubt." Wols, who committed suicide in 1951, is known now as a herald of the informal abstract painting of the fifties.

Consider also some words of E. Rosenthal, author of a small collection of essays about modern art. Rosenthal sees new freedoms and great possibilities as a result of modern psychology, beginning with Freud. But within this very framework he also deals extensively with man and the insecurity characteristic of modern art, for example that of Paul Klee. "Fear is something we find everywhere in modern art, and it is directly related to hellish feelings which have their origin in the unconscious," wrote E. Rosenthal. Maybe the best definition of the work of these artists is found in Holbrook Jackson's description of the work of a predecessor, the English poet Davidson: "The strife of the artist for a new expression, a new poetical value, is too evident . . . the courage and the honesty of a mind valiantly beating itself to destruction against the locked and barred door of an unknown and perhaps nonexistent reality."

Never has freedom been discussed so frequently as in our times; in itself perhaps the best indication that freedom itself has been lost. Buñuel knows this. Others, to their despair, know it too. Does not Sartre speak of man being sentenced to freedom, when he asks whether the freedom which man has to take upon himself is not a curse, and itself the greatest lack of freedom? Over and over again, implicitly or explicitly, freedom and the lack of freedom are the issue confronting us when we focus our attention on modern art. Have not fear and despair, the realization of being caught in a world which in essence is bad and rotten, everything to do with the loss of human freedom? Are they not the very signs of its loss?

We must return here to Genesis 1: God created a world which was good. Then came the Fall, and with it both judgment and redemption. Sin, the fruit of desire, came under judgment and led to death. Salvation from this misery came from God himself, first in the promise, and then later in its fulfillment in Christ. But no matter how deeply sin has penetrated the world and defiled it, man has remained man and God's world the creation, and the norm retains its value. Because of our shared humanness, we can understand something of what moves man in our times to promise himself and others freedom, while in reality he is the slave of corruption—not just in a theological sense or according to a Christian interpretation, but according to his own experience and words (2 Peter 2:19).

In the first chapter of this book, I have talked in much greater detail about the two lines in history: the line of Cain and Lamech, and the line of Seth and Enoch. These two lines are responsible for two types of culture.

All culture is the fruit of human activity. Man is driven by motives deep down in his heart to shape life on the basis of the way he understands it. In the line of Cain, culture will be the fruit of unbelief; in the line of Seth, it will be the fruit of belief. Unbelief produces all the horrors—sin, hatred, and death—which we find summarized in Romans 1 (see also Isaiah 5:15, 16). Yet because man remains man, he can never go to the utmost limit. Neither Sartre nor Buñuel can lead the life they preach about. Buñuel himself cannot even bear to kill an animal. What is it then that keeps him from breaking through his godless ideas and accepting reality? The answer is simple: he is caught in sin. We must realize that the words of Paul, which say that in Christ man can be freed from the law of sin and death (Romans 8:2), are true not only in the pulpit, but in the totality of life, and thus for cultural matters as well. Artistic leaders need Christ's liberation just as much as anyone else.

The Decline of Western Culture

The truth is the same for everyone. The church has often forgotten this. In the words of G. J. Dippel: "Why is the church the way she is? Because in the church the same pseudo-myths of cultural and social behavior are honored as they are in the world. . . . The same ideas seem to manifest themselves, the same unacknowledged presuppositions. . . . No matter how much the church twists itself in innumerable coils of Christendom, she misses her basic assignment when she refuses to call culture, politics, and public opinion to repent. . . . This is the only meaningful form of revolution open to man. This is the revolution which calls for . . . the giving up of those false securities which have led to death. Western humanity is threatened by the products of her own hand, based on wrong securities and customs."

The revolution which Dippel describes means abandoning faith in the things we call obvious, which on weekdays fill us with more confidence than the certainties we profess on Sunday. Are freedom from or slavery to the law of sin and death indeed matters that affect "normal" reality?

Let us look first at our Western world, the world we have to live in, and consider the fruit of the Reformation in our Western culture. As one fruit we must certainly mention the Counter-Reformation—the renewal and purification of the Roman Catholic Church. A second fruit would be the stimulus to humanism, which although it claimed its roots in classical antiquity, was essentially something different. A third fruit was renewal in the moral and social spheres after the restrictions of the Middle Ages. A fourth fruit was the artistic freedom which came when art became unshackled from the Church, and artists were freed to discover new frontiers in their work.

It was during this period that our Western culture as we know it was built, a culture which although far from perfect, was also a fruit of faith. Of course, people were sinful in those days, but at least there was a consensus, a general agreement about norms and morality and an understanding of reality such as has rarely been demonstrated in history. There was richness, openness, and freedom, grounded in the reality given by God at the creation, and therefore neither sectarian nor private. Tragically, all too soon the world of the Counter-Reformation was marred by absolutism and the dreaded Inquisition, and freedom was destroyed.

Meanwhile humanism was attempting to deepen its foundations, supporting its attempts to reform the world on such theories as those of Descartes. In the eighteen century, the humanistic and cultural thrust of the Enlightenment found little resistance from Christendom, weakened as it was by mysticism and traditionalism, as well as by the corrupt absolutism with which the Roman Catholic Church tried to maintain its position alongside the secular power of the monarchies.

The cultural influence of the Enlightenment stemmed from the declaration of humanistic man that he no longer needed God. Only very gradually were the consequences of this new mentality realized. First the whole structural consensus of Western culture as it had been developed during the preceding centuries had to be broken down, a process which has happened so slowly that it is not complete even today. But we can see now more and more clearly, particularly in art and philosophy, the fruits of this new tendency based on the conviction that God is dead and man is free to build in his own strength.

We have chosen Buñuel's film as a twentieth-century example of this process. To grasp the nature of this new culture, we may simply consider the issue of freedom, which is, after all, a broad concept. First, driven on by a positivistic approach to reality, man studied his own life and actions to find the basic laws of his being; was man *really* any different from animals and nature? The result was that man found himself inescapably caught in a determinism growing out of his own positivistic world-view, and thus trapped in the technocracy about which so many books have been written!

Still, man remained man. He tried to retain his freedom and fought desperately against this mechanistic philosophy. Modern art is one of the most eloquent testimonies to this fight, as is existentialism, which has submitted the human predicament to an exhaustive analysis.

Human freedom, assert the existentialists, exists outside of, beyond, alongside technology. Perhaps man is no more than an atom, but he knows about his existence, his "being." He knows that he is a "being unto death" *(Sein zum Tode),* and in this knowledge lies his opportunity to transcend his "thrownness" *(Geworfenheit).* "Thrownness" is a term invented by Heidegger to describe the situation of mankind as "thrown" into a world which it cannot comprehend and which it had no share in making. Man achieved a kind of freedom in this way; he had desperately looked for it and passionately affirmed it. But it was only fragmentary freedom, gained mainly by declaring the greater part of reality to be senseless. The consequent dialectic between nature and freedom is inhuman and unpalatable. So modern man tries once more to escape and grasp again his true full humanity.

This situation, complex but concrete, affects not only philosophers, but also many young people. Awareness of it helps us to understand some of the things that are happening in our world, the tensions and stresses in the field of culture and science, and even the conflicts in the personal and family life of thousands. We can understand the rebellion of Buñuel and his sympathizers; they cannot accept the situation, but know of no way out. In their desperate search for freedom, modern writers and artists have tried to break through all the norms and structures of life. But the end result has been a still greater lack of freedom, so that many find themselves asking whether even art itself has not been lost.

More than once I have been asked—and not only by "bourgeois" Christians—whether all mainstream modern art is not in essence like Hans Christian Andersen's story of "The Emperor's New Clothes." One is tempted to sympathize with this question, but to answer yes is to pose another problem: how do people get into a situation so devoid of freedom that they think they see clothes where none exist? How else can we describe the horrors of modern drama, and films like *Un Chien Andaloux?* How else does the work of a Raysse get into a museum? Almost inescapably, these modern works present themselves as fruits of the modern attitude toward life.

Our Basis for Art

Art can flourish only in and from freedom. And it can gain warmth and joy only from love, not hate. Our task as Christians should be to work on the basis of the freedom which we have gained in Christ's redemption. We must ourselves be creatively involved. Far too often we are content to watch the activity of the world—admiring, amazed, or irritated! We must look for positive ways to express a true vision of reality, and in searching for new forms we can breathe life into them so that they bring joy to our needy contemporary world.

But, first of all, we cannot do this in our own strength. Any Christian work which is begun without looking to the living God for help, strength, and insight is doomed to powerlessness. We must never forget Jesus' words that apart from him we can do nothing good or meaningful (John 15:5, 6).

Secondly, when we ask for Christian activity in the arts, we are *not* calling for a sectarian style, the art of a subculture. We ask for art that is fully art, which springs from the fullness of what we are, and which takes into account the whole reality in which we live, a reality immeasurably greater than simply the total of nature plus man. Such art will express joy and beauty, it will give honor and praise—but it will never close its eyes to sin and misery. It will be, in short, an art born of the freedom given to man by God. Art should be a form of play, rejoicing before the face of God (Proverbs 8:30).

Thirdly, nobody could imagine that the road we have just described will be easy and smooth. Men do in fact long for freedom; but because they prefer darkness to light (John 3:19), enmity—or at least resistance—will be in store for us. We could go into this in more detail, but a reference to 1 Peter 3 must here suffice.

Fourthly, artistic freedom is a human freedom, that of a creature, and therefore not absolute. It was only from the Fall on that man longed to be equal with God. Our freedom exists within the human limitations laid down by God. Without a norm for life, there would be no point in talking about art or beauty; they would mean nothing without some regulating structure.[5] Paul in Galatians 5:23 mentions the fruit of the Spirit; "against such things there is no law." This certainly holds for artistic norms. It is only when we try to break the norms that we lose our freedom. The advice in Philippians 4:8, 9 to think about those things which are "true . . . honest . . . just" (KJV) in no way hinders our work. On the contrary, it opens the whole world before us.

Some Dangers to Freedom[6]

When we talk about freedom, we usually mean freedom *from* something. One freedom we still have in the West is the freedom to produce art independently of political or other coercive social influences. This is the legacy of seventeenth-century civilization. Everyone knows how this freedom has been threatened in the twentieth century. We should not think here only of Nazi Germany or Soviet Russia, but also recognize the dangers of a politics of subsidies, however well intended. We must really defend artistic freedom, demanding it even for works which we may not approve of.

Again and again, fearing that freedom might be misused,

the church has tried to tie Christians to new laws. Christians have recoiled from Paul's passionate appeal to live out of the freedom in Christ, arguing, "We never know where things may end up." This legalism is the weakest point in modern Christianity, a striking proof that God's laws are wiser than man's. And it is exactly here that the world, including Buñuel, most violently attacks the church. Christian freedom is not lawlessness, but it is openness, the right to realize all the potentiality of our talent. Paul spent his life defending this freedom—he felt it basic to the Christianity he preached—and this in itself proves that even in those days, men found it difficult to live by faith in the finished work of Christ and by trust in God. Men always want to play it safe, and Christian leaders with the best intentions repeatedly tend to replace freedom with legalism. There are pharisees in every age.

Freedom should mean liberty to experiment, to walk in new paths, and even to make something which goes against the ideas of a former generation. It also means the latitude to make works of art that are not perfect. Some critics may be long-suffering, but the rigid ones and especially the moralists should understand that perfection cannot be demanded—not immediately, at least! Such a demand cripples spontaneity; perhaps this explains the remarkable dearth of artistic activity within the church. To grasp freedom is to take a risk. God himself took a tremendous risk when he placed man in creation *with* his freedom. And in spite of its misuse since the Fall, God still preaches freedom, through the mouths of the prophets and apostles, and through Christ himself (John 8:32). Are we not trying to make ourselves wiser than our God if we refuse to take the risks implied in the freedom he has given us?

Freedom also liberates us from every historically conditioned cultural ideal. It is ridiculous to maintain that at any given time man can work only in such and such a way, if what he does is to be meaningful and to the point. We are never completely bound within a particular situation, although of course we cannot live totally outside it. We need never be dominated at a given period by one style or manner; there are always other possibilities and other answers. Historicism, which says that man is caught within the norm of his own time, kills every kind of free creativity. I think we see this in our own time, when so many feel obliged to follow the latest fashion and the most way-out art. This is mere snobbery and shows a lack of courage to accept the responsibility of freedom.

We are free to choose whatever subject matter, style, or technique we find useful; free to be traditional; free to try something entirely new; free to illustrate biblical stories, or noble ideals, and free to focus on the smallest flower. The art historian of the future may perhaps be able to trace where the tradition came from, what was the source of the new art; he may even find that something truly new has emerged. But the artist should not be worried by fear of future art critics. The artist should be driven by what seems appropriate and sensible at a particular time.

The artist also needs the freedom to create art which is connected to life. One of the strongest disagreements we have with modern art is its belief that the artist is a prophet, and art a kind of revelation. This kind of thinking has been responsible for many modern works which are not so much works of art as arguments in a kind of theological debate, often of a nihilistic or anarchistic character. Little inspiration seems to come from the reality in which the artist lives. As in the case of Buñuel, his surroundings seem a long way from the setting he depicts in his films.

Modern art is supposed to be autonomous, but there is an impoverishment, a loss of freedom, when we cut art loose from its ties with life and place it in a vacuum, a kind of scientific laboratory. The full reality of human life is infinitely removed from the "reality" of modern gnosticism. There is no need, every time an artist makes something beautiful, to rap him over the knuckles saying, "Don't you know about the atom bomb, about Vietnam, about the injustices of our society, about our country's heartless bureaucracy?" We are not saying that artists should never portray evil, and depict the unreal and the sentimental. But a nihilistic theology offering a counterfeit reality cannot be forced on us for no better reason than that it is the style of our time. We can achieve a much deeper and better understanding of reality than those who speak of *échec* and *nausée*.

What a gulf there is separating *Un Chien Andaloux* from, for example, the blues of the American Negro, those "songs of sorrow and frustration." When the black man sings "The sun rises in the east and goes down in the west, you never know what is best," he is using poetry to express a troubling situation; but he evokes a compassion seldom achieved by Buñuel.

The Christian artist must not be misled by the spirit of the age with its anarchistic lack of freedom. He should investigate everything while retaining the good (1 Thessalonians 5:21). This will lead him, perhaps unwittingly, to function as salt, inspiring others to work out the full meaning of their true humanity, unrestricted by a narrow philosophy or theory. It has always been the task of Christians to unmask pseudo-gods or false ideals and to reopen a vista towards the fullness of reality.

This is not an invitation to look nostalgically back to some golden age of the past. Instead we should have our eyes focused on the future in the hope of a fresh, new vision. We must beware of traditionalism, and instead accept our responsibility towards the future on the basis of a living faith.

We started our discussion of Buñuel by asking whether what he showed was, in fact, reality. We conclude by saying that if the Bible is true, then Buñuel is wrong. The strength of Christianity lies precisely in the fact that it offers joy in the midst of suffering because of its certainty that justice will finally come. It knows that evil has *already* lost the battle and will eventually be totally defeated—not by men who may have good intentions, but by the living God through the work of Christ Jesus (see Romans 8:18ff.; 1 Corinthians

15:20ff.). We must therefore take hold of the freedom that Buñuel has lost. It is the freedom to love our neighbor, to perceive creation as beautiful and fascinating, and to reckon life worth living.

CHAPTER SIX

Does Art Need Justification?

A NEW SECULAR RELIGION?

Somewhere between the Middle Ages and our times, art became Art. The visual arts had always been understood as a craft, even if a very special craft. In the fifteenth century, however, and specifically since Giotto, the position of art began to change. Artists began to aspire towards more recognition, hoping to see painting take its place with poetry, scholarship, and letters and even be introduced into the circle of the seven liberal arts. Some great artists like Rafael, Leonardo, Michelangelo and Dürer nearly achieved this status, but for lesser artists it was out of the question.

In the eighteenth century, however, art finally took its place as a form of "high culture." To be an artist could mean to be a genius, one of the great leaders of humanity, a seer, a prophet, a high priest of culture. Art with a capital A even came to challenge the place of religion, itself becoming a new religion in a secularized world. Also, the term "culture" took on a new meaning, separate from the natural sciences, economics, and technology. (Someone who is favorably inclined might say that culture involves high human pursuits, removed from the practical things of daily life. Someone less sympathetic might call culture a pastime for the rich, or the *nouveau riche* middle class. Expressed negatively, culture has no real meaning at all, and is the hobby of a snobbish coterie.)

For the few really great artists, this change was no obstacle. They came to be revered as superior people, their works sold and discussed in the learned and cultured circles. For the vast majority of artists, however, the change was almost disastrous. Although their profession was regarded as high and important, and surrounded with the aura of Art, often their works could not live up to such a high standard. Certainly a less prominent artist could not survive on the income from work regarded by most people as inessential. Art was something to look at or, in the case of the musician, to listen to or, in the case of literature, to read. Visual art especially was certainly not something to spend much money on. As a result, many artists were very poor, and even important works could not be produced without high subsidy. Now art, or Art, has become elevated and refined, but must be kept alive in a highly artificial way. (Note the implications of the very term "*art*ificial.")

Another result of the present situation is that along with Art, a new kind of artistic category has emerged, a type of work which is confined to the realm of the crafts, but which is often not recognized as valid primarily because most artists of quality tend to despise it. We refer here to popular art, which is often called "commercial" or "entertainment" art. To entertain seems to be one of the great sins in art. Yet, if we hold such a position we are challenged by the quality of a waltz by Johann Strauss or the jazz of Duke Ellington; and in commercial art there are such outstanding figures as Toulouse-Lautrec and Cassandre.

Not only the artists, but art itself has suffered from this shift. Placed too high in the total culture, art has lost its ties with reality, and therefore its meaning. Abstract art is one result of this change. Also, because art has taken on religious significance, it has given birth to some very strange offspring. As a result, art has for most people become an esoteric activity, extremely intellectualistic on the one hand,

and fostering irrationality on the other. It has become confined to the museum.

A museum is a place where one usually finds objects which have lost their function in contemporary life. The modern art museum, however, has almost become the nihilistic temple for an anti-religion. In a way, this is also true of the museums of the older arts, like the Metropolitan Museum in New York or the National Gallery in Washington. "Cultured" people know the famous works of art in order to refer to them just like Christians quoting Bible texts.

As a result, people have come to examine the true meaning and function of art. What is art, really? What is its importance? Why bother with it at all? Certainly in teaching, one must deal with these pertinent—or should we say impertinent—questions. And many answers have been formulated. Art teaches us deep things. But, say some, art should not be didactic; it is meant to enrich life. Is art, then, only for the rich, or for snobs? For those who have the time, the money, and that peculiar gift called artistic sensibility? Can art never be for the toiling, hard-working men and women, or for those who live far from all cultural centers? Oh yes, most people do have paintings on their walls, but that is only decoration; one could certainly not call it Art. Art is too high and special. Indeed, art has become something lofty and removed, and even the interpretation of art has become a strange and difficult pursuit, since one must read into the works meaning that is certainly not evident to the "unenlightened" masses.

The elevation of art to its current position is in itself a sign of the crisis that exists. High Art has become strange and esoteric; popular art, with which most people are surrounded, is often very low in quality, revealing and even promoting the spiritual poverty of our age.

This crisis makes life very difficult for many artists and art students. For many, art has become a gratuitous activity. Nevertheless they continue, often searching for their own identity in their work, like the philosopher depicted by Max

Klinger: a man looking in a mirror at his own image.[1] Art is said to be an expression of man's innermost being.

But what if there is nothing inside? The artist is supposed to be a genius, and geniuses cannot be taught. Young artists are frequently left to themselves, to find themselves and their own forms of expression. They often reach a point of despair; but when they cry for help, they are thrown back upon themselves and many crumble under the load. Unless one is really strong and endowed with great talents, or filled with a powerful ego-drive and able to carry off a profitable program of self-promotion, success in the art world will elude him.

A HEDONISTIC PASTIME?

Art is in crisis. This is no less true in the Christian world, where perhaps the crisis is even doubled. On the one hand, Christians are children of their own times; on the other hand, they tend to regard the arts as the very epitome of the non-Christian spirit of our age. Two different responses then follow: either one abstains from the arts altogether, and leaves them to the "worldly pagans"; or one enters the art world, hesitantly and with many questions and doubts. Each of these positions requires some justification.

The justification of the first attitude may be that after all, man's real calling in life is to be a witness for Christ and to live the "spiritual" life. And since art does not enter this realm, it can be ignored. The interesting thing is, however, that having taken this attitude, one cannot really avoid art. For having discarded art, one still uses a stained-glass window in the chapel, or one illustrates an evangelistic pamphlet or church paper, using either "old" art (like a copy of a Holman Hunt painting) or popular art. That the pamphlet therefore looks cheap does not seem to bother anyone. After all, the message is the only thing that counts!

The second attitude, that of the Christian who does enter the art field, is often difficult to defend in the face of the first. "Isn't it sinful to devote a life to the arts, which are worldly anyway, only for giving pleasure?" Many a Christian who is active in the arts is made to feel like a kind of hedonist, someone who never works (art is not work!), and who is in constant danger of falling into the evil snares of this world. Usually he is seen as a person of strange or impractical ideas. After all, what has art to do with the realities of daily life, especially "Christian" daily life?

Many fine Christians who have a talent or an interest in the arts are forced to defend their involvement by saying that art is an excellent means of evangelism. When art is used as a tool for evangelism, it is often insincere and second-rate, devalued to the level of propaganda. I would call this a form of prostitution, a misuse of one's talent.

A GIFT OF GOD

Art is not a religion, nor an activity relegated to a chosen few, nor a mere worldly, superfluous affair. None of these views of art does justice to the creativity with which God has endowed man. It is the ability to make something beautiful (as well as useful), just as God made the world beautiful and said, "It is good." Art as such needs no justification; rather, it demands a response, like that of the twenty-four elders in Revelation who worship God for the very act of creation itself:

> You are worthy, our Lord and God,
>   to receive glory and honor and power,
> for you created all things,
> and by your will they were created
> and have their being. (Revelation 4:11)

The supreme justification for all creation is that God has willed it to be. And so there is no need to justify, let us say, a tree. A tree is there and is meaningful because God made it. Of course a tree has many functions: birds sit on its branches, cattle rest in its shadow, and men use its wood for building houses or making fires. What would the world be without trees? Yet even if the tree is indispensable to many ecological cycles and useful to mankind, none of these functions alone, nor even their sum total, can provide the justification for and the meaning of the tree. The tree has meaning simply because God made it; that meaning surpasses all its functions. If we do not see this, we are not far from accepting naturalist evolutionary theories, which are all based on functionalist assumptions.

God's creatures require no justification. God has given them their value by including them in the totality of his creation. In the same way, our personal human qualities and activities need no justification. To love is indeed a command of God, but a justification for it is not given. To marry, to praise the Lord, to till the ground, to prepare meals, to talk, to feel, to think—all need no apology within the context of "Hallowed be thy name, thy will be done."

In the same way, art needs no justification. It is meaningful in itself, not only as an evangelistic tool, or to serve a practical purpose, or to be didactic. Art must be free: free from politics (including church politics); free from traditions of the past, free from mode of the present, free from the judgment of the future; and free from our economic and social needs. Art cannot be turned into a mere function of any of these without losing its indispensable place in human life. After all, Christ died for us in order to restore our humanity, and to give meaning back to God's creation. Not only is evangelism Christian, but all of life is Christian, unless we would make Christ very small.

But if art needs no justification, it also does not follow that art is to be art for art's sake. Just as a tree, being more than the totality of its functions, nevertheless *has* functions, so art is not just there to be art, but is bound by a thousand ties to reality. Nothing is simply autonomous. A tree, a human being, a work of art—all are part of that wonderful fabric which we call reality; no thread can be missing without impoverishing the whole.

So even if art has meaning in itself, it can never be on its own. It would wither and die. It is tied in two ways to reality. On the one hand, art deals *with* reality; it is *about* fear, hope, joy, love, our surroundings, the things we love or hate. On the other hand, art is used *in* reality. Music, rhetoric, poetry make up a large part of our social functions and religious activities; and architecture, furniture and textile design, interior decoration, painting and illustration provide the setting for our movements and actions.

No matter whether art receives a prominent place or serves in the background, the fascinating truth is that the more it becomes engaged in reality, and the more concrete its manifold ties with our daily life, the more we will recognize that it needs no justification.

APPENDIX:

Letter to a Christian Artist

Diemen, The Netherlands
August 23, 1966

Your letter reached me yesterday after its trans-Atlantic voyage, and I propose to answer you directly. Your request touches on a problem I have been thinking about for a long time. Maybe what follows can be of help to you. I'd like to approach the matter in a schematic way, pointing out some principles.

Your questions concern your wish to paint—that is, to work as an artist—as a Christian. It really is remarkable that you decided to do this when you were just converted. Many times new Christians just drop their artistic careers because they think painting and art today are incompatible with being a real Christian. I'm glad you made this decision and hope to help you by suggesting the following principles for Christian artists:

1. If God has given us *talents* we may use them creatively—or rather, we *must* use them creatively. A Christian artist is not different from, say, a Christian teacher, minister, scholar, merchant, housewife, or anybody else who has been called by the Lord to specific work in line with his or her talents. There are no specific rules for artists, nor do they have specific exemptions to the norms of good conduct

God laid down for man. An artist is simply a person whose God-given talents ask him to follow the specific vocation of art. There may be circumstances when love towards God would forbid certain artistic activities or make them impossible, but the present moment in history does not ask for such a sacrifice. Quite the contrary. We—the Christian world and the world at large—desperately need artists.

2. To be God's child means to be offered *freedom*—the Christian freedom Christ himself and Paul in his letters say much about. This freedom is most important for anybody who wants to do artistic work. Without freedom there is no creativity, without freedom no originality, without freedom no art, without freedom even no Christianity. This freedom can exist only if it is based on love towards God and our neighbors, and if we become new men through the finished work of Christ and the Holy Spirit is given to us. Without this base, freedom may easily mean being free from God and consequently free to indulge all the cravings of the sinful heart of unredeemed man. (For more on this matter of freedom, see Paul's letter to the Galatians.)

Christian freedom is different from humanistic freedom, the freedom man gives himself to build a world after his own devising (as was tried by the Enlightenment and the humanist development after that time in the Western world). Humanistic freedom leads to all kinds of problems, as our Western world is now learning from experience. Freedom in the biblical sense is in no way negative—shun this, don't do that, you must leave that alone, keep away from this. Christian freedom has nothing to do with a set of rules by which you must bind yourself; indeed, such rules may easily be pseudo-Christian. Freedom is the necessary basis for creativity, for creativity is impossible when there is timidity, when you allow yourself to be bound by narrow rules. Do not think the modern art world is free—but we will turn to that later.

Freedom is positive. It means being free from tradition, from the feeling that everything you do has to be original, from certain fixed rules said to be necessary in art—but also from the thought that to be creative you must break all kinds of rules and standards.

Freedom means also that there are no prescriptions for subject matter. There is no need for a Christian to illustrate biblical stories or biblical truth, though he may of course choose to do that. An artist has the right to choose a subject that he thinks worthwhile. But nonrepresentational art provides no more freedom than the most involved allegorical or storytelling art.

Freedom includes the right to choose your own style, to be free from tradition but also from modernity, from fashion, from today and tomorrow as well as from yesterday. Yet there is no need to slap the contemporary in the face, as some streams of art nowadays deem necessary. Christian freedom also is freedom from the sinful lust for money, from seeking man's praise, from the search for celebrity. It is the freedom to help a neighbor out and give him something to delight in.

3. There are *norms for art* that are a part of God's creation. Without them art would be an empty name without sense. To say a person has been given a feeling for art and beauty (everybody has, to a certain extent), that he has been granted a strong subjective sense of artistic rightness, is but another way to say that he has been given an understanding of certain norms God laid down in his creation, the world in which we live. We call this *taste,* a feeling for design and color, the ability to grasp the inner harmony of a complex of forms and colors, the understanding of the inner relationship among elements of the subject matter, the ability to recognize the indefinable dividing lines between poor and good art, between worn-out symbols and fresh ways of saying things that are important to man.

These norms do not stand in the way when we want to live in Christian freedom; they are a part of our world and our nature. Only when man revolts and does not want to be a creature, when he wants to be God and not man, does he feel bound by these norms. For those who love the Lord and rejoice in his good and beautiful creation, these norms provide the opportunity to live in freedom and to create. As one cannot act and live free as a woman if one is not a woman and has not the nature of a woman, so the norms for beauty and art are at the same time the opportunities to see beauty and create art.

4. When God created—and in that way made the perception of beauty and the human creation of art possible—he gave art (or any artistic endeavor) a place in this world in which we live; and that world he called good. (I added artistic endeavor because we have to think not only of the rarefied museum type of art called Art with a capital *A* today, but also of all other types, including ceramics, dance music, pictures used in Sunday schools, and so on. We shall come back to this.) Art is here because God meant it to be here.

So art has its own task and meaning. There is no need to try to justify one's artistic activity by making works with a moralistic message, even if one is free to emphasize moral values. Nor is there any need to think one has to serve as a critic of culture, or always provide eye-openers to the non-artists, or teach, or evangelize, or do whatever other lofty things one can think of. Art has done its task when it provides the neighbor with things of beauty, a joy forever. Art has direct ties with life, living, joy, the depth of our being human, just by being art, and therefore it needs no external justification. That is so because God, who created the possibility of art and who laid beauty in his creation, is the God of the living and wants man to live. God is the God of life, the Life-giver. The Bible is full of this.

Art is not autonomous. "Art for art's sake" was an invention of the last century to loosen the ties between art and morality; that is, to give art the freedom to depict all kinds of sins as if they were not sinful, but simply human. The human understanding of depravity, of morality, of good and bad was thereby undermined or erased. The results we are seeing today, in our century. The meaning of art is its being art; but it is not autonomous, and it has thousands of ties with human life and thought. When artists cease to consider the world in its manifold forms outside the artistic domain, their art withers into nothingness, because it no longer has anything to say.

Much abstract art today is art, yes; but it has little meaning because it is *only* art. All its ties with reality have been cut. This applies as much to a ceramic product as to a painting. Art has its own meaning and needs no excuse. But it loses its meaning if it does not want to be anything but art and therefore cuts its ties with life and reality, just as scholarly work loses its importance and interest if learning is sought for its own sake. Art and science become aestheticism and scholasticism if made autonomous. They become meaningless idols.

The artist's work can have meaning for the society God put him in if he does not go to live in the ivory tower, or try to play the prophet or priest, or—turning in the other direction—in false modesty consider himself only a craftsman. He has to make art while thinking of his neighbors in love, helping them, and using his talents in their behalf.

5. Most art today expresses a spirit, *the spirit of our age,* which is not Christian. In some ways it is post-Christian, in others anti-Christian, in still others humanistic. Here and there are Christian artists who try to do their work in a godly spirit. But often their brethren leave them alone, distrusting their creativeness or doubting that they are Christians. False art theories that have pervaded the Christian world—the artist as an asocial being, a nonconformist in the wrong sense, a dangerous prophet, an abnormal being who lives in an alien world—are often responsible for this attitude. But some Christian artists themselves hold these false views and look down with contempt at their fellow-Christians. Anyway, there is a lot of confusion.

That the art of the world at large is also in a deep crisis does not make things easier. We live in a society where there is a break manifest between the mass of men and the elite, and another break between the natural sciences and technical realities on one side and religion (most of the time rather mystical) of a completely subjectivistic and irrationalistic type on the other. We who live in this world cannot act as if these deep problems did not exist.

There is *no real Christian tradition* in the arts today to turn to. If an artist wants to work as a Christian and do something that he can stand for and bear responsibility for, he has to start with the freedom based in a true faith in the living God of Scripture. He has to make art that is relevant to our day. Therefore, he has to understand our day. And, in order to gain from all that is good and fine today and yet avoid being caught by the spirit of our age and its false art principles, he must study modern art in all its different aspects deeply and widely. He must try to analyze the language modern artists use, their syntax and grammar, in order to be able to hear correctly the message they profess to speak. To analyze, understand, and criticize lovingly, loving man but hating sin, in order to avoid their mistakes but gain from their achievements—that is the Christian artist's task. A new Christian tradition, as a fruit of faith, can grow only if artists who understand their work and task, their world and its problems, really set to work.

6. But what has the Christian artist to offer the world? He has *a freedom to do something*, not just the freedom for freedom's sake. What should he aim at? Let's be careful not to lay down new rules. There are no biblical laws that art must be realistic or symbolic or sentimental, or must seek only idealized beauty.

The artist as a Christian is free, but not with a purposeless freedom. He is free in order to praise God and love his neighbors.

These are basic laws. What do they mean in practice? May I refer, this time without comment, to Philippians 4:8—"Finally, brethren, whatsoever things are true, whatsoever things are honest, whatsoever things are just, whatsoever things are pure, whatsoever things are lovely, whatsoever things are of good report; if there be any virtue, and if there be any praise, think on these things." Here we read what a Christian standing in freedom as a new man, in God's strength and with the help of the Holy Spirit, must search for. This also applies to the Christian as an artist. It is up to him to work, to pray, and to study, in order that he may realize as much as he possibly can of these truly human and life-promoting principles.

In the Lord,
H. R. Rookmaaker

Part Three: Creative Sharing of the Gospel

CHAPTER SEVEN

Communicating the Gospel to Modern Man

Over the years, in L'Abri Fellowship and elsewhere, I have talked to many young people coming from a wide variety of backgrounds. Often they have asked me what I thought about evangelism, whether there were principles to go by or methods to follow. In this chapter, I should like to consider some questions that are often asked, and suggest some principles for communicating the gospel to others.

OUR POINT OF CONTACT

A Christian Is Human

Being a Christian is not a matter of wearing blue earmuffs with polka dots. It does not mean wearing red socks, or putting on a false nose. How often the world thinks, "There go those Christians! He is a decent fellow, and she is friendly. They may go to church on Sunday and pray before meals; but thank goodness, they're pretty normal otherwise."

If this is all it means to be a Christian, then we are indeed only ordinary people with an extra something added. Just a little strange, a bit odd in some ways. If this is the way we want to witness, then there is no point in even beginning. What should make a Christian different from other people is that he is more fully human, more what God intended man to be when he created him. Not someone with odd rules that only isolate him from his neighbor, or beliefs that have nothing to do with daily life, but seem appropriate only for the soul, the future, or for the crises in life.

The gospel is more than a mere opinion, a personal discovery, or something our fathers or forefathers dreamed up. It is the *truth*. Only so is it worth talking about.

Furthermore, the Bible which contains the gospel is very definitely not a religious book or a collection of devotional texts. The Bible is about reality, and has something to tell us about life and relationships today. As such it is our standard, the basis of our practical and intellectual decisions. It is crucial that we remain willing to submit our words and actions to its correction.

Know the Other's World

In telling others about Christ, we must keep in mind whom we are speaking to, and be familiar with his world. Paul said we must be a Jew to the Jews and a Greek to the Greeks. Many misunderstand these words to imply a compromise, as if we should think and act just as the other man does, and then hope he will be prepared to listen to the little extra we have! But Paul is talking about something completely different. He spoke to Jews very differently from the way he addressed the heathen on the Areopagus at Athens. Because of their different backgrounds and occupations, their knowledge and the framework of their thinking, they had different interests which had to be taken into account.

Therefore, just as missionaries have to learn the language (which involves some knowledge of background and mentality) of the country they are sent to, we too must learn to speak the language of the other man. Like the "Jews" or "Greeks," our neighbor has his own language—even though we may both speak English. When we say, "God says this" or "God says that," what does our listener understand by the word "God"? The Supreme Being? Nature?

There are many gods in this world, but they are utterly

different from the God of Abraham, Isaac and Jacob, the Father of Jesus Christ. We must make clear who God is. Otherwise, when we speak of him our neighbor may have a totally different idea of God in mind. We must be sure that all our terms are understandable to the other person; this involves a genuine sensitivity to the framework of his thoughts and feelings.

For example, a person who has been brought up as a Christian may find it quite obvious that man is sinful. But if a Christian uses the word "sin," he cannot be sure what others associate with the word. Even if they see it as something very terrible, it still may not be what we mean. Nor does it really help to use a statement from the Creed or the Authorized Version of the Bible. These may have a certain connotation for churchgoers, but the language is likely to be incomprehensible to our neighbor, seeming to come straight out of the Middle Ages!

We should, moreover, never begin evangelism by discussing matters that are secondary to the gospel itself, like church attendance, the Christian way of life, or the ecumenical movement. It is of no use to talk of these things to someone who does not yet know God. Witnessing is not advertising; our goal is not to get members for our church, our community, our cause. Our message is not for the benefit of institutions we hold sacred, but for people.

A Different World-view

Modern man has a radically different world-view from that of the Christian. Man's understanding of the world and of himself has profoundly changed, particularly since the eighteenth century. I am not talking here about theories or intellectual ideas far removed from life. Modern man's world-view is the result of many generations of teaching during which certain assumptions and principles have come to form the foundation of his outlook on almost everything. Although he may not know the names of the great philosophers past and present, his starting point when thinking about man is humanism, and his presuppositions about nature are derived from the natural sciences. Even the present crisis in humanism itself and the failure of science to provide adequate answers to life do not drive him back to God, but make him turn (skeptically perhaps) to the most recent modern movements in the scant hope that they may offer a way out of his dilemma.

In his life-style and goals, modern man is very different from us as well. This does not necessarily make him wrong; on some points he could well be right. (Sad to say, it has often not been Christians, but unbelievers who have taken the lead in issues like ecology and the energy crisis.) We must get to the very basis of modern man's thinking and see what can hold before God within the reality he has created.

It is no use closing our eyes to the world-view of the unbeliever. We have to be open. We must be willing to put our insights and knowledge to work, and to study. Contemporary Christians who know nothing, for example, of Marxism are neglecting a vital area of the battle. If they fail to understand the Marxist position, they will never be able to discuss with Marxists, nor answer the problems they pose.

Modern man is aware of the world's many injustices and hypocrisies. He sees oppression, abuse of power, and the economic dictatorship of big business. If he blames Christianity for these things, we must not defend the present order by pretending that it is Christian. We must stand alongside modern man against the decay and downfall of our Western world. But we can also show him what has gone wrong, and that true deliverance can be found only in Christ, who died to make a better world possible.

Indeed, a great strength of the biblical message is that it is directed not only towards the individual, but also to the community and the nation. The gospel is for every nation, tribe, people, and tongue (Revelation 7:9). Some Christians have forgotten this.

Christianity is not a mystical consolation to help the individual escape daily reality. Instead, it urges us to go even deeper into reality, which has been created by our Father. This is why I stress that we must be so careful with our use of certain words. We preach a real Christ who felt real anger at injustice, greed, and hypocrisy, and who died on a real cross.

It is difficult to communicate with the truly modern man, who is often to be found among the working classes and the intellectuals. As a result, many Christians have given up trying to reach either of these groups. We have been reaching only the middle classes, those who still have some knowledge of Christianity and are willing to sit in a stadium with thousands of others and listen to a comforting old message. But in spite of difficulties in communication, modern man will have to stand before God one day to be judged and see the results of his sin. If we have not warned him, God will require his blood at our hands (Ezekiel 33:8; 1 Corinthians 10:11).

"The Silent Majority"

Many of our contemporaries are not really "modern men," but what we could call bourgeois; they are part of the "silent majority." These are the people who want to avoid the gloomy conclusion that unless something drastic happens, our society will soon be finished. They believe in man and want to live a "normal" human life. Optimistically they insist that even if the present is not very rosy, man will still be able to build a great future. After all, have not new times of prosperity always emerged after periods of crisis? The bourgeois man wants to be happy, and his gods—small but powerful—are money, sex, and comfort. But the bourgeois man has no real basis for his optimism, and he pays a high price for his comfort—namely real life, real humanity.

What are his standards? Maybe he stands for law and order—after all, there are so many crooks who may try to rob him of his security and his ease! Even if his basic philosophy is not so different from modern man's, he tries to avoid seeing the consequences, the death and the dirt. He closes his ears to the groans of the poor and the oppressed—though he may occasionally give money to charity to ease his conscience.

The bourgeois has no consistent standards. What stops Mr. Smith from committing adultery? The danger of being found out. (What would happen to his career? What would the neighbors think?) He tells his son to dress neatly. Why? Because of what the neighbors might say. But if neighbors represent the only norm for life, then the son is likely to say at a certain point: I will do as I please; I will dress as I choose and go to bed with the neighbor's daughter. This is his protest against the pragmatism, the utilitarianism of his father who has only practical reasons for not committing adultery. There are many such sons—and daughters—today.

Bourgeois people lead a very normal life. They have a few children. They go on vacation. They receive a gold watch after twenty-five years on the job, and a pension when they reach sixty-five. After that, there are a few years in an old people's home, and finally the grave. We must admit that Christians are often like this. That is why the protest of modern man has often been aimed at Christians—not only because of their bourgeois ways, but because they have failed to provide any alternatives.

An old Beatles' song describes Eleanor Rigby, whose task it is to darn the minister's socks. Finally one day she dies. The minister buries her and washes his hands. "All the lonely people, where do they all come from?" Why do Christians keep their mouth shut? Have we nothing to say? We should be concerned for these lonely people, and also for the bourgeois who have lost the way of life.

I speak of them as bourgeois rather than as middle-class, because in this sense of the word many intellectuals and working-class people are also bourgeois. The bourgeois man is even harder to reach than the modern man. Modern man knows about the lostness of this world, but the bourgeois tries to deny it. All the songs of the protesters cannot shake him out of his comfort. He even manages to harvest some fruits from the protest culture, making money from pop music and posters.

We must certainly not preach the bourgeois an "easy gospel" that satisfies his spiritual cravings, fills his emptiness, and even offers him security in the next life! A mystical type of Christianity, stressing that all worldly things will pass, only gives him false security. He feels confident that he can live what he calls a "normal" human life—he even has a foundation for it. But the gospel is truth, not a psychological tranquilizer! Becoming a bourgeois to the bourgeois means telling him that his dreams are legitimate, but that ultimate peace and happiness cannot be found by closing one's eyes and ears to the evil in the world.

Modern artists and thinkers have also tried to wake up the bourgeois and make him see the world as it really is. Martin Esslin, writing about the modern theater of the absurd, says:

> There are enormous pressures in our world that seek to induce mankind to bear the loss of faith and moral certainties by being drugged into oblivion—by mass entertainment, shallow material satisfactions, pseudo-explanations of reality, and cheap ideologies. . . . Today . . . the need to confront man with the reality of his situation is greater than ever. For the dignity of man lies in his ability to face reality in all its senselessness; to accept it freely, without fear, without illusions—and to laugh at it.[1]

The Christian would agree about the bourgeois, but never tell him to laugh at his lostness; that would be cruel. Better then to let him sleep.

We must make the bourgeois see that this world is in turmoil because of what mankind has done. We are not just discussing "secular" matters, but events that can be understood only if we see in them the active working of God. Isaiah 9:18 describes the situation: "Wickedness burns like a fire." Yes, what man does is destructive, but God adds to this (verse 19): "By the wrath of the Lord Almighty the land will be scorched. . . ." As Revelation teaches us, when Christ opens the seals and the trumpets sound, judgment will come over a world which has turned from God. Nevertheless, there is hope. It is possible to return to the Lord in repentance, with a genuine hunger to see justice done. This goes far beyond merely seeking to save one's own soul, and is the heart of our message to the bourgeois.

Lost Man Is Still Man

Everyone is searching for humanity and truth. And everyone lives in the same world as the Christian, bearing God's image. This is the point of contact between the Christian and the man of today. We must never forget that the other man is also human. Perhaps sometimes he wants to forget that himself; he tries to say that humanity means nothing and that love is only sexual attraction. But in his heart he knows this is not true.

At this point I would like to tell a true story that took place in the fifties. A boy and girl, students of Jean-Paul Sartre, were sitting on the left bank of the Seine, weeping. Why? Because they loved each other, and wanted to express their love. But they had come to believe that the words "I love you" meant only "I have a sexual urge." False reductionist theories had told them that love was no more than a bourgeois facade meant to give respectability to the animal instincts of procreation. And so they wept, because they were denying what their experience told them was true—that love does indeed exist.

This couple, like many other people in our modern world, could not abandon their humanity, and their tears were a protest as well as a sign of despair. Though truly persons, they were unable to live as such. Men long for humanity, because they *are* human. They cannot explain sin, but know that it is there and sense that it brings death. Truly modern men have begun to realize that they cannot create a better world with their knowledge. They perceive that in spite of their great knowledge, they have destroyed everything.

As Peter Gay has said:

> Eighteenth-century thought had liberated man from his filial dependence on God and made him part of nature, but the philosophical anthropology of the philosophes (like Diderot), which promoted man from servitude, ironically enough demoted him at the same time—from his position little lower than the angels to a position among the intelligent animals. While man seemed on the point of conquering the worldly domain through his critical intelligence, he was faced with a second expulsion from his terrestrial paradise, and this time the avenging angel was man himself.[2]

Yet leftist theorists and activists continue to long for a better world. They point out injustices like the heartless use of money and power, the manipulation of desperate people by propaganda, and other destructive practices in our society.

Indeed, modern man acknowledges many injustices. But he no longer understands that sin originates with disobedience to God and a lack of love towards one's neighbor. That the abuse of money and power, corruption and crime are not recognized as sin may even be the basic mistake, a sin in itself, whereby man continues to talk "objectively" about the structural ills of society. I do not mean to say that such structural faults do not exist, but more is wrong with the world than just organizational or sociological weaknesses. Sin goes deep and defies analysis. And unless sin is "cured" at a very deep level (which is what Christ came to do), all human endeavor to better society is in vain.

Men long for an ideal world, and to realize such a world they are willing to sacrifice both freedom and human lives. But in their hearts there is despair. Knowing that humanity is not won this way, they still try, even against all odds. They keep hoping that man himself can be changed if the order of the world is altered.

We must admit that there is validity in their longings, and even admire their persistence. If God did not exist and

Christ had not come as the supreme Protester—One who would not accept this world full of sin and death, but was and is able to do something definitive about it—then we too would feel compelled at least to try to make a better world ourselves, even if deep inside we knew the effort was hopeless.

Our contemporaries' craving for justice proves their humanity, and we may add that it is Christianity which has made man aware of the injustices. Without the preaching of the gospel, the leftist ideology—which is in effect a secularization of the gospel—would not have existed.

Why then are so many modern activists anti-Christian? Because Christianity has often forsaken its calling, and followed the ruling powers. Because Christians have accepted existing injustices. But also, let us add, because some Christians who have done more than most people realize may not call attention to their own good works. And finally, because history taught and studied for two centuries from a humanistic, secularized, so-called neutral point of view has made us forget what the Lord has done and what fruits faith has brought forth. We overlook the spiritual force that motivated the reformers, and have learned to explain their works in terms of social and economic forces and natural circumstances.

The fact remains, however, that most leftists are not optimists, but are basically existentialist in their outlook on man. They—at least the deeper thinkers—know that a Savior is needed. They know what is good and true because all reality testifies to it, including their own humanity. But the terrible truth is that, knowing what they do, they still are not converted (Revelation 9:20, 21). They know they are forfeiting their humanity; yet, rejecting God's solution, they still seek answers in places where they cannot be found, and continue on the road to final lostness. Paul describes this in the first chapter of Romans (verses 18 and 19), where he speaks of men who by their wickedness suppress the truth. Like all sin, this is incomprehensible. For sin takes away freedom; it destroys; it relegates mankind to an unnatural and broken world that lacks the very things men yearn for.

The situation in which we speak the gospel to our fellowman is critical. But in the midst of almost insurmountable difficulties, we also find the point of hope that because the other man is searching for humanity, we have something in common, a basis for communication. We can talk about good and evil, life and death. He will certainly know what we are talking about. And we can tell him what God has meant humanity to be, and what it still can be if we live as God's creatures in the open world which he has given us.

These things are not mere theories. Modern films and modern books (even pornographic ones) show that sin—man's quest to be free to indulge in lust and to search for happiness—is inevitably linked with disillusionment and death. Through it all echoes a scream of anguish. Man is caught. He can find no adequate answer, unless the vicious circle is broken by true redemption as he bows before the Creator and Savior whose words give significance to life.

Summary

Today man is indeed caught in a vicious circle. We have already referred to the dilemma of the bourgeois man. His mentality, often marked by a Victorian morality, leads to the antibourgeois protest: Don't you see you are no more than a cog in the machine, a number in the computer? This is true reality. Your morals have no foundation—science has long ago disproved them. How can you go on living as you do?

But even the protesters themselves gradually realize they cannot accept man as nothing but an object of nature. They cry out for freedom, identity, humanity. But by then they can no longer discover what is true, for truth consists only in what science can prove.

Rebelling against this, modern man tries to find his humanity by leaping into the area of existential freedom; he wants to jump out of the box of technology in which he is caught, only to find that even this little bit of freedom is an illusion. Some, like Timothy Leary and Allen Ginsberg, have extolled LSD as the open door to the mystical experience of freedom. Ironically, however, this "freedom" is dependent on a technological product: a pill. But even Leary and Ginsberg were saying nothing new. In the twenties Aldous Huxley wrote *Brave New World,* which describes a beautiful new world—beautiful, but unlivable; drugs were needed to make it bearable.

The use of drugs is further evidence that reality and humanity without a reference point are too much for modern man. He is willing to sever his contact with reality, to reduce his own consciousness of it, in the hope that it will become less of a burden. This, however, is an escape, not a solution.

Why does man go on in this way? Because he is man, and cannot stand still; he strives for real humanity. Our message to him must be that true humanity can be found only in the gospel.

Sometimes people finally do get to this point, only to discover all too often that Christians, individually and in the church, have reduced humanity again to something bourgeois. They are disappointed when they come up against a bourgeois Christian, for it means that Christianity has lost its flavor, its saltiness. Bourgeois Christians say they believe, but live as if faith were nothing but religion, valuable only for the future life.

Our task, our calling, is to be human. Life has meaning, and love for our neighbor is possible. Our certainty lies neither in ourselves, nor in nature; it lies in God, with whom life is an adventure.

We must let others see the consequences of their own point of view. We must show them how they have thrown away their humanity. We must tell them that God has a real answer to these questions, and that he, too, has no use for a lukewarm church (Revelation 3:16).

SOME BASIC QUESTIONS

There are some specific questions that non-Christians often ask, good questions which we cannot with honesty avoid. The present form of these questions may be different from that of the past, for modern man is influenced by modern thought-forms. But the questions as such are not new; they come back in every age, and are the very questions which the Bible answers.

I once had a Bible study with some thoughtful non-Christian students. They were existentialists. As I started with Romans 1:18, they began to ask questions. The amazing thing was that these were exactly the questions which Paul answered in the process of his own discourse. Sometimes the students even used almost the same words! As we continued, not only did they "reconstruct" the whole letter up to Chapter 8, but they also began to see that Paul was dealing not only with his contemporaries, but with questions for all time, concerned as they are with the nature of man and the world.

Here are some of the more recurrent questions, together with the main thrust of the biblical answer. It is most important to be clear about the nature of evangelism. Evangelism is not telling someone what a wonderful experience of Christ I have had, nor even what he has done for me. It does not mean saying, "Look at me; am I not wonderful!" and thus hoping indirectly to show something of the Lord. No, it is instead standing alongside the non-Christian as a fellow sinful human being, also needing a Savior. Then one can share the good news that the Savior has come. Our Christian life is, at best, a means to show that what we preach is a reality.

Can We Be Sure That God Exists?

In one way, the answer to this question must be no. Even if all his creation points to him, God is not part of it, nor of the things that man can see, understand, or experience. People often ask this question because they want the kind of proof which modern science would give. However, the approach to reality which accepts only those things we can weigh, measure, or perceive with our senses will never lead to a proof of the existence of God. Indeed, the entire modern system of rationalistic thought was constructed to exclude God from this world, or at least from those things which scientists considered worth thinking about. There is no way to discover God by means of a system which deliberately denies him! God does not exist in the same way as the world exists; he is the Creator of that world, of all that exists, the Maker of existence itself.

It is preposterous for man to try to prove God. Rather, it is man himself who has to be "proved" before God. Today people try to prove theories in order to put their knowledge to use in practical ways; science and technology are closely related. One could conclude in this context that if we were able to prove God, we would then be able to manipulate him! This would perhaps be possible if God were lower than man, if he were impersonal—a kind of immense powerhouse. But we know that God the Creator is a personal God, a God who lives. In biblical terminology, he is also a jealous God who is not going to share his place with any other god, and certainly not become the servant of a new god called man.

We should never try to answer someone when he asks whether God's existence can be proved. God is the Father, and his Son is the way, the truth, and the life. They cannot be put on a level with anything on earth that man tries to prove, whether a biological hypothesis, a sociological theory, or a philosophical speculation.

A quite different question is whether we can see God's work, his actions. Here the answer is yes. Just open your eyes, if they are not too dimmed by sin, prejudices, and the excuses men use to escape considering who he is (Zephaniah 1:12).

Man's doubts of God's existence are almost absurd, for he has given a full and overflowing revelation in the Scriptures, where we find not only his words, but his actions in history. He reminds Israel again and again: "I am the Lord your God who brought you out of Egypt." And there is so much more. The Scriptures are full of the objections of God that he has sent his servants, his prophets, in vain and that men have refused to listen to him and tried to live as if he did not exist (Hosea 11:1-4). Man will never receive a fuller answer about God than that given to Job: "Where were you when I made this world?" Men want a sign, but Christ said that the only one they would get would be his resurrection. The sign, in our midst for centuries, has been evaded ever since (Matthew 28:11-15).

If men can no longer see God, it may be because he is indeed hiding himself; but if so, then this is itself a judgment (see Isaiah 57:17 and Micah 3:5ff.).

If God Is a God of Love, Why Did He Make This World Full of Sorrow and Suffering?

God's original creation was not a world full of pain and death; it was good. But the Evil One tries with man's help to turn it into a horrible chaos. Nevertheless—and this is most important—God cannot accept the sufferings of men, women, and children. When people talk about the evils of the world, they almost always mean the big things: war, famine or pestilence. Often they forget the sufferings of everyday life: unkind words, lack of love or freedom to communicate, lack of hope—all the many thousands of so-called "minor injustices."

God does not forget them. And he is angry. Christ, the supreme Protester, was incensed when he saw all these things (see, for example, Matthew 23). When man protests, his words are feeble because he cannot really alter things, and his attempts often make the situation worse. Christ, however, was not only angry; he was able to *do* something.

This is the very heart of Christianity. Christ came to

change things. He came, he died, he rose again from the dead, and his great work has continuing effects, described both in 1 Corinthians 15:20ff. and in Revelation. If our protest is right and honest because our hearts are filled with sorrow, then we share the mind of Christ, whose protest was motivated not by defiance, but by love.

The recent activities of extreme leftists, like the protest movement of the sixties, have shocked many people, who cannot understand why others have rejected the beautiful world they are trying to build. But Christians can be shocked only if they have failed to hear the cry of the oppressed, the weak, and the poor—the wretched of the world. Non-Christian protesters are much closer to where man should be than are bourgeois optimists who keep hoping that everything will turn out all right in the end.

If God Is Good, How Can He Accept the World As It Is? Why Does He Not Put an End to Evil?

This question is closely related to the last, and has already been touched upon. Certainly we must empathize with its urgency, for the Bible itself is full of the cry, "Awake, O Lord! Why do you sleep? . . . Rise up and help us; redeem us because of your unfailing love" (Psalm 44:23-26). The same cry is heard in the New Testament, as in Revelation 6:10, where the martyrs cry to God to avenge them and restore justice.

The Bible assures us that our cry is not in vain, and that God indeed acts in the world. First Corinthians 10:1-4 is one of many biblical passages that remind us of this. However, it often seems to us to take very long before some things are corrected. That is because God in his patience wants to give man the opportunity to change. We must wait expectantly for the day when justice will finally prevail (Psalm 73:17ff.). God hears the cry of the martyrs' blood and the groans of those who suffer unjustly, and will come in his glory to set everything right.

The thought of the Last Judgment fills many people with

fear, but we should remember that it will be a great day, a day when order will be reestablished, and no act of cruelty will pass unnoticed; the balance will finally be restored. We are told to look forward to that day, and pray that it may come soon. God is waiting for many to be added to the number of those who have been forgiven in Christ and will stand in glory on the new earth (Revelation 7:9-17).

How Can a Loving God Bring Judgment Over Man?

Interestingly, this objection is the exact opposite of the last one. It is precisely because God loves that judgment must be. Love is not something soft and sweet. If God had said he was sorry that man had fallen, but then gone no further, it would mean that he cared neither for man, nor for his creation. There would have been no gospel, for the heart of the gospel is that God made the world and is still interested in it. Therefore, God must come with judgment, for he is the only one who can put a stop to evil.

Judgment is not an arbitrary act, unrelated to the things man does. Judgment is a way of cleansing and preserving this world. Moreover, when God sent death as a part of the curse, he put a check, a limit, on sin and evil. As a result, man can never become totally degenerate; he knows how vulnerable he is, especially to death. The other side of the coin is that evil itself is never allowed to grow to complete fruition (Romans 8:19ff.); mankind and creation have been spared its full consequences.

If one loves something, one cannot bear to see it destroyed. God loved his creation, but he also loved man and wanted him to be what he was originally created to be. He could not settle for a lower standard. If there were no judgment, we should have to accept man as being less than he really is. If we love man, we cannot do this.

We should turn the argument around and see that we human beings often underrate sin and evil; we just do not see their seriousness. While we talk flippantly because we are indifferent, God's imminent judgment shows that to him at least the world is of much more than casual importance. Reality is more than we realize; man's every thought and action are significant. This should fill us with awe.

If the Claims About God's Omnipotence Are True, How Can Man Be Responsible? Can Man Have Real Freedom?

Indeed, this is beyond man's understanding. We cannot understand how God is three and yet one; how Christ can be fully God as well as man; and how there was nothing, and God spoke, and there was. Yet these things are not irrational or absurd. It is true that although we may grasp the meaning of these words, we will never be able to explain them fully. How could anyone explain how God created and maintains the world? How is he able to set the times and the seasons while simultaneously allowing so much freedom everywhere that man is even able to turn against his Creator? We cannot explain these things, but how could they be otherwise? Our knowledge and experience testify that God really is the great God he claims to be, and yet we are free. We can do what we like, including evil, within the framework of human limitations and options.

The trouble is that we compare God to ourselves. We can create things, but they are always determined, bound by our designs, our programs. Think, for example, of the computer. God, however, is the great God he is precisely because he was able to create a universe in which all things move in freedom, and yet without chaos!

This particular question is really the age-old one which all philosophers have tried to answer: the problem of freedom and determinism. All recognize that both exist, but no one can explain how. Even the Bible does not try. It is just beyond man's understanding. We should have to be on an equal level with God and comprehend his depths if we were to know the answer.

We also face this question in our own human experience. The Bible refers to it, without trying to account for everything in an all-embracing theory. I am thinking here of the wonderful words of Paul, which are so true to the believer's experience, and yet so inexplicable: "Work out your salvation with fear and trembling, for it is God who works in you to will and to act according to his good purpose" (Philippians 2:12, 13).

Because He Is Finite and Restricted, Man's Achievements Are Less Than Perfect. Is This Imperfection Sin?

We humans are restricted. In spite of our freedom to choose, we have certain limitations because of the kind of creatures we are: we cannot swim like a whale or fly like a hawk. We are also limited by time and space: we cannot be in two different places at the same time. There is nothing wrong with these limitations, for they were also part of man before the Fall. Only God is infinite and unrestricted in his power.

However, this question could indicate that we are still bound to the sinful wish that led to man's fall: the wish to be like God. Man wants to do those things which God said were wrong, and which go against his own nature. Ever since the Fall, man has constantly done things that oppose his own freedom, his own understanding and love (Romans 1:18, 19; 7:21). Our creaturely limitations, given when God made us, are not wrong or sinful. We do wrong when we refuse to be what he has made us.

But happily this is not the end of the story, for our deliverance in Christ means not only that he has forgiven our sins, but that he has conquered the evil in us and set us free to become what he originally intended. The gospel has restored our true humanity (Colossians 2:9-15).

PRINCIPLES OF PERSONAL EVANGELISM

Having dealt with some of the questions about Christianity which we can most frequently expect from non-Christians, it is important to discuss some of the main principles we must keep in mind when communicating with them about our faith. These principles are also relevant to our own total Christian life and understanding of the world.

We Ourselves Cannot Convert Anyone; Only the Holy Spirit Can Change Hearts

It is our responsibility to give honest answers to honest questions. We cannot expect others to believe us just because we have strong convictions, nor ask them to take a leap in the dark.

The responsibility of sharing our faith is overwhelming. We cannot convince anyone; who are *we*? That is why we must accompany every discussion with the silent prayer that God will convince the other man; perhaps the Spirit will lift the veil of the unbeliever's sinful wish to suppress the truth, and allow him for just one moment to look reality—even his own reality—right in the face.

Jesus, speaking of his disciples' difficult confrontation with possessed people, said, "This kind can come out only by prayer and fasting." Fasting means being willing to sacrifice something, to set some things aside for the sake of one's petition. In his words in the upper room, described in John's Gospel, Jesus says more about prayer: "Soon I will go away, but understand that I do these things because there is a three-way bond between the Father, myself, and you. I do these things because I love you, and I love God. This is all done in order that your prayers may be heard" (John 14:13ff., my paraphrase). John's Gospel repeats this five or six times. Jesus died not only to forgive our sins, but also to make us new people. He died so that our prayers might be heard, including our prayers for our neighbors.

Imagine that your boss, a humanist, is coming to visit you one evening. Before he comes, you might pray, "Lord, guide our conversation so that we may have a chance to talk about you. Let him see that the Bible is not out of date, and that the gospel is concerned with the ordinary events of life." Once you look behind another person's mask, you may discover many difficulties. It may be possible for you to talk about one of these problems, and to give an answer. God can use such a visit to build his Kingdom, but not without prayer. When Christians realize their dependence on God in these matters, great things can happen.

The Lord does not, however, answer all our prayers immediately. Sometimes we may have to wait, perhaps because we ourselves need to learn something, or because the other person must learn to trust us as real human beings. Whatever the reason, we must not give up too easily.

Our Faith Is Not in the Bible Itself, but in the Lord Who Reveals Himself Through It

Christians should not put all their trust in the Bible; it cannot be their god. Our faith is not in words, nor in commands or parables, but in the living God. The reality of God, who rules this whole universe and a great unseen world of which we know next to nothing, is too immense to be contained even within the Bible.

Christianity is certainly a "religion" with a book, but that book is not simply the story of a cult, nor a collection of devotional poetry. God has used the Bible to tell man about himself. The Bible speaks primarily of the reality of this world, of the God who lives, of a Savior who really exists and who accomplished something on a real cross not just for the souls and feelings of men, but for the world in all its fullness. Because Christianity deals with reality, it is not only for Christians that these things are true.

To Accept the Biblical Message Is Not to Deny One's Intellect

Bultmann and other theologians have said that to accept an unaltered biblical message in our day would be a sacrifice of the intellect. It is indeed true that we have many things today that did not exist in biblical times: television, cars, airplanes. But these things do not undo the truth of the Bible, nor make it obsolete. It is true that our modern thought-forms are often not in line with those of the Bible, but perhaps it is modern man himself who has sacrificed his intellect and lost the way to understand the world. We have limited our horizon to what we can understand and know with the help of our human brains and senses.

The Bible, though far from supporting rationalism, is not contrary to reason. It does not ask us to believe strange things far removed from all human experience. Can a woman bear a child without contact with a man? No, says the Bible, this never happens—only in one case, and this is therefore a once and for all exception. Can a man return from the grave? No, says the Bible. Only Christ was able to overcome death, because he was also God; his resurrection was an exceptional event.

Can miracles happen? The greatest miracle is the wonder of God's creation. But can a man walk on the water, or heal the sick? Can fire come down from Heaven as happened during Elijah's sacrifice on Mount Carmel? Why should a man not be able to walk on water if that man is the Son of God? If God, the Lord of creation, wants to show that he *is* Lord by sending fire from Heaven, why should that be strange? Such a happening would be strange if he did *not* exist; but since he does, would it not be peculiar if he were unable to do these things? The Bible is not unreasonable here. There may be some things in the Scriptures we cannot explain, but they are never against reason if we first acknowledge the great God who has revealed himself. Part of believing in God is recognizing that he has the power to do what we in our own strength are unable to do.

The Bible does not ask for a sacrifice of the intellect. It begins to be inexplicable only when I insist on denying all the things which I cannot actually see in the world around me. Even in biblical times these miraculous things were not common. Just count the number of people who ever saw an angel (and their amazement when they did!). If God did not come to Abraham, how was it possible that so many years before Christ he believed those great promises for the future of his folk—believed because God had told him so? If the things the Bible relates did not occur, how did the Bible itself come into existence? The very unity of its message and the events it describes are surely comprehensible—even if the message could never have been conceived by man (Isaiah

55:8, 9). By accepting the Word of God we begin to see and understand, for the fear of the Lord is the beginning of wisdom.

Again, how can the Bible be false when on so many pages it asks us to inquire, to look, to investigate for ourselves whether the events it describes are true, or coming true according to prophecy? (See, for example, Matthew 24; Luke 1:1-4; John 2:22; 20:27-31; Acts 1:3; 4:20.) If the Bible is not true, then Jesus was an impostor, a liar, or at best a fool misleading himself by making such great claims. How can people say that Jesus was a great man, and at the same time deny his claims to be the God-sent Messiah? If the Bible is not true, then according to its own standards we had better call it a strange and impossible deceit. Can we really imagine the apostles sitting down to make up the story that Jesus rose from the dead, or constructing legends to create propaganda for a dead idealist? What would they have to gain? Most of them lost their lives for what they said. And certainly the period that elapsed between the things that happened in Jesus' time and the first gospels and epistles is too short to allow such a legend to gain credence. Also, the idea that the Old Testament is full of "prophecies" written after the events occurred creates more problems than it solves; the Bible's plain message is easier to accept. Psychologically, historically, we run into great problems as soon as we try to deny the veracity of the biblical witnesses.

To Accept God Is Much More Than Merely to Believe That He Exists or That the Bible Is True

The question that modern man so often asks about the existence of God is closely tied up with epistemology, for it asks the question in the terms in which it was formulated during the Age of Reason. As such it is a wrong question. It is also unanswerable; God cannot be put on an equal level with the realities of his creation. God's existence is so abundantly clear from all creation—even apart from the Scriptures—that it is hard to deny his being. Of course, without

Scripture it would be difficult to say anything positive and precise about him; that is why we need revelation.

A positive answer to the question of whether God exists is only a small step toward truly following him. One does not become a Christian by believing that God exists—the devils know that, too (James 2:19). To be a Christian means that we love him and want to follow him even if it proves costly and difficult.

We should accept the Bible as God's revelation if we want to be his followers. But saying that the Bible is true also does not make us Christians. We are not only to accept the Word as truth, but to *do* the truth (John 3:21). It is not enough just to say yes to a system.

Love Is the Only Legitimate Motivation for Evangelism

Our calling is not to tell about the church, nor about ourselves or our experiences. It is important to emphasize this because of the many misunderstandings which exist. The only reason I talk about Jesus is because I love my neighbor. My neighbor is not just modern man in general, but much more specifically John with whom I work, Mrs. Smith next door, or the man sitting opposite me in the train. Am I going to condemn them to be lost because I am too wretched to speak? Because I love my neighbor, I want to help him and pass on freely what I have received from God.

The following story sounds almost like a caricature, but it really happened. One day a young man offered to help an elderly woman cross the street. As he accompanied her home they got into conversation, and she told him how she had once belonged to a church, but because of her husband she had given up attending. Now that she was old, she had begun to think of these things again. All the young man could say was, "Isn't it a bit late to ask for the address of the true church?" A response like this is totally without love. Nothing can happen if we lack love.

Some Christians evangelize in a legalistic way, only to

fulfill their duty, their witnessing all too often sounding like a phonograph record—grinding out the same lines and slogans without any real interest in the person before them. They pay no attention to his questions, his problems, his personal situation. It is a sin to do missionary or evangelistic work legalistically. As Paul says in Galatians 2:15ff., we are no longer subject to the law. This is not just a theological statement, but a truth we can accept with great joy.

The only reason for telling other men and women about Christ is that we know it will be good news—an answer to their personal needs. Christians should love their fellowmen, whose need of God is just as great whether they are criminals, or immoral, or just people of another type or class than themselves. Christians are sometimes very harsh to people whose lifestyle they find low or degraded. It is as if they have not read what the Lord said about the harlots, the wicked and the poor who needed him and should therefore not be sent away, but helped. The same is true of unbelieving family members. Our guide should not be what others think, but what the Lord says, and he told us to care for the lost.

Whenever we see someone destroying his life through sinful foolishness, we should weep. At the same time, we must understand that he can really change only through the work of the Holy Spirit. Only after Christ himself has become a person's Lord and Savior can we try, carefully and tactfully, to lead him in a more godly way of life. A new Christian will often need our help to show him gently what the Lord asks of his followers—not a whole string of do's and don'ts, but true fruits of the Spirit.

Evangelism Cannot Be Limited to One Method or Approach

Because people are different, and their backgrounds and experience vary so enormously, no one method can reach everyone. We can never communicate if we do not reach people where they are. What is right and appropriate in one situation can be totally inept in another. This makes life fascinating, but it is also why methods can be so deadly. If, however, we are driven by love, the Holy Spirit can show us how to act.

This does not, however, mean that study is unimportant. On the contrary, we must have knowledge of the other man's world if we are ever to make meaningful contact with him. And of course we need to study the Bible in order to know what we are talking about. Although we shall never have complete knowledge and know all the answers, we have no excuse for being lazy. Without such study, it is dishonest to ask the Holy Spirit to lead us, for God is too great to be used as a kind of servant to carry out the things we have failed to do.

In our own lives, meanwhile, must be evidence of the fruits of the Spirit. Otherwise, we cannot honestly claim that Christ has overcome evil. The Bible says that anyone who claims to be God's child, but goes on sinning is walking in darkness (1 John 1). This does not mean that we must be perfect; we shall all continue to need forgiveness. But some change in our lives must be apparent.

Not Everyone Is Called to Be an Evangelist

In many Christian circles, evangelism is seen as the first and probably most important task of the Christian. I do not agree. The Bible does make clear that whenever we are asked about our faith, we must give an answer, and not deny the Lord by acting as if we do not know him. There can also be no argument as to whether the church, the body of Christ, is called to proclaim God's message. A Christian community that is not interested in the furtherance of the gospel is in need of careful self-examination.

This does not mean, however, that every Christian is called to be an evangelist, or that there can be no Christian life without direct acts of witness and testimony. Some people are called by God for this special work, and in answer to prayer he gives them particular talents and opportunities. But not everyone is called to be an evangelist. Many Christians are deeply frustrated because they have been told that the first law of the Christian life is to evangelize, and yet they do not know how to go about it. They feel inadequate, and the Lord never seems to give them opportunities. Their frustration is the painful result of a hard legalism, and it is unnecessary.

Like the Old Testament prophets, some people in the New Testament—like the first apostles and Paul—are specifically called to preach the gospel. But we never hear of a general command to all of Christ's followers. Paul exhorts his congregations to live a good Christian life; but as sharp as he could be in pointing out their shortcomings, he never rebukes them for not evangelizing. He also does not command them to do so, but explicitly states that God has called him and other specially appointed people to do that demanding job.

A Christian can bear fruit for the Kingdom of God in many ways. There are rich variations in our callings. One may be a scholar or technician, a housewife or teacher, a musician or painter, a bookseller or a farmer. Those who are not evangelists or preachers, theologians or missionaries are no less Christian than those who are. Nor is their work unrelated to the gospel. In this day, marked more and more by the absence of a Christian lifestyle, we find that honesty, truthfulness, reliability, wisdom, and insight into the basic truths about human life are becoming ever rarer. We have the opportunity to show clearly that what we do is different, and that our goals are not conformed to those of the world around us.

Everyone is called by the Lord to "full-time Christian service." We are God's children twenty-four hours a day, or we are not Christian. But full-time service can be in the kitchen, at the helm of a boat, doing accounts, helping sick people, or looking after the plumbing system.

We can also say this in another way. Paul speaks about the Christian community as a body, made up of various members (1 Corinthians 12). If we compare the evangelist with the mouth, it becomes obvious that more is needed to make a whole body. Perhaps your calling is to be a foot, an ear, an eye, or even some less conspicuous member. We cannot all be evangelists, as there must be a body behind the evangelist—helping him with money, with prayers, but also with insight and knowledge, maybe by analyzing the spirit of the modern age, or by making the building or decorating the interior of the room he speaks in. Also, if the evangelist is to speak of new life in Christ, he must be able to point his listeners to a living church made up of real people. There ought to be cooks, teachers for the children, musicians, caretakers—a wide variety of people, each of whom helps to complete the body of Christ. How can we do without them? Let us not build a surrealistic and absurd church, made up only of mouths.

We can sum up all we have been saying in one sentence: Christ did not die merely to make us Christians. He died that we might be human—men and women in the fullest sense of the word.

THE DANGER OF CHRISTIAN UTILITARIANISM

Having understood these things, we must beware of the danger of Christian utilitarianism. This is a most appalling trap, into which one can easily fall. If we believe evangelism to be the ultimate and only real Christian work in the world, this means that any other work must be second-rate, and at best only an aid to evangelism. Art—fine, but what can it do for evangelism? Business—nothing wrong with it, provided it can be utilized for evangelism. Why do we live?—in order to evangelize. We smile, not because we are happy, but because we want to be regarded as happy Christians. And so on. This means that all these things, which are gifts of God, lose their intrinsic beauty and are prostituted for evangelism.

If the supreme purpose of art is no longer to sing the praise of the Lord and be a joy to our fellow-beings, but to provide a tool for evangelism, we soon do not ask whether art is good and beautiful, but only whether it can be used to convert people. We are then not far from trying to manipulate the people we want to reach. Another trap is to give the people merely what they want; art is not seen as important in itself, but only as a means of carrying a message, and the artist is asked to do things that fail to meet the best standards. Music, graphic art, other forms of communication are dragged down to a level of mere usefulness for evangelism, but fail the test of honesty, beauty, and integrity.

Art has its own value. The music of Bach, for example, is certainly Christian, but it was not composed to attract a large crowd to be preached at, nor to stir up emotions so that people would more easily accept the message. The music of Bach, and the art of Rembrandt, are in themselves a witness because they show what it means to adopt Christian standards, to use one's talents in order to make the very best work one is capable of; this in itself honors God. Call it preevangelism, if you like.

Here is a challenge for us, the challenge to show that the end never justifies the means. We must not sacrifice our honesty, failing to make quality work because we fear it may not appeal to popular taste. In the very act of denying our own standards, we also insult the human beings we want to reach, as if they cannot see through our cunning little devices. I have spoken to many people who have been hurt, and estranged from Christianity, in this way. I have also seen Christians distressed because they wanted to find a place where the Bible was really taught, but heard only evangelistic talk in the churches they went to, talk which led people no further than conversion.

WHAT IS AN EVANGELIST?

After all we have said, we must not forget that the Bible does assign a particular role to the evangelist. What does it mean to be an evangelist? How does his work differ from that, for example, of a missionary?

The missionary is a man (or woman) sent to a country, a

people, a nation that does not know the gospel. He must bring the Good News into a society and culture completely molded by a non-Christian religion and mentality. Yet he must be careful, while preaching God's message, that he is not simultaneously introducing Western culture, an especially important consideration at a time when Western culture itself is in a state of crisis and has drifted from its former Christian foundations. He cannot be a proponent of Western supremacy, for anything that indicates a colonialist or racist mentality will be detrimental to his work, and will contradict God's message that all are in need of salvation, regardless of racial or social position.

The evangelist has a quite different task. He addresses a Western world that has heard the gospel, a culture that once was Christian but is now falling into apostasy. (Hosea 4:1-3 describes the situation perfectly, even including pollution.) Everywhere people are ignorant of the Word of God; they think they have "come of age" and do not need it. The position of the modern evangelist differs only superficially from that of the Old Testament prophets. The prophets were speaking to the Jewish people, who had received a specific call from God, but were often far from God-fearing. In the midst of their heathen practices, they dared to believe in continuing peace and success. The prophets called them back to God, quoting passages from the law to warn them that if they did not put an end to their greed and idolatry God would come with judgment, concrete and inescapable. However, the prophets also preached that God is a God of mercy; there is a chance for the individual to return, though he must be prepared to face social pressures and perhaps even persecution. In such circumstances, God has a special message for him (see Jeremiah 45 and Zephaniah 2:3). The prophets also spoke of a way of return for whole nations, a way which could lead to blessings instead of the threatened afflictions.

The same warnings and promises apply in our age. Today's evangelist is the prophet of our time, speaking to people who have forsaken God, the Giver of so many blessings. The twentieth-century prophet needs to study the prophets of the Old Testament, and echo their call to repent: Repent and accept the true God; give up your wrong philosophies and false religions. Stop suppressing the poor and the socially weak. Stop putting financial security and personal happiness before the glory of God. Reject dishonesty as a part of politics. In short, turn from the modern mentality in all its ungodliness. The words of Micah to his generation could not be more timely:

> With what shall I come before the LORD
> and bow down before the exalted God?
> Shall I come before him with burnt offerings,
> with calves a year old?
> Will the Lord be pleased with thousands of rams,
> with ten thousand rivers of oil?
> Shall I offer my firstborn for my transgression,
> the fruit of my body for the sin of my soul?
> He has showed you, O man, what is good.
> And what does the Lord require of you?
> To act justly and to love mercy
> and to walk humbly with your God. (Micah 6:6-8)

NOTES

Chapter One

1. See Chapter Three of this book, "Creativity in Love and Freedom."

2. Thomas Carlyle, *Sartor Resartus* (St. Clair Shores, Mich.: Scholarly, 1977).

3. See Chapter 5, in Os Guinness, *The Dust of Death* (Downers Grove, Ill.: InterVarsity Press, 1973).

Chapter Two

1. Popma, *Philosophia Reformata* XXXVIII 1973, pp. 103, 104.

2. *Ibid.*

3. *Ibid.*, p. 110.

4. Allen Ginsberg, "Howl," from *Howl and Other Poems* (San Francisco: City Lights, 1956).

Chapter Three

1. John Cage, *Silence: Lectures and Writings by John Cage*, (New York: Wesleyan University Press, 1961), p. 195.

2. Martin Esslin, *The Theatre of the Absurd* (Garden City, N.Y.: Doubleday, 1961), p. 316.

3. *The Heidelberg Catechism*, Question 54.

4. R. E. D. Clark, *Christian Belief and Science* (London: English Universities Press, 1960), pp. 27ff.

5. Charles Darwin, *Autobiography and Selected Letters*, Francis Darwin, editor (New York: Dover, 1892).

Chapter Five

1. Feodor Dostoyevsky, *The Brothers Karamazov,* Chapter 35 (New York: W. W. Norton, 1976).

2. Jean-Paul Sartre, *Huis Clos* (Englewood Cliffs, N.J.: Prentice-Hall, 1962).

3. Henry Miller, *Tropic of Cancer* (New York: Grove, 1961), pp. 256, 257.

4. *Ibid.*

5. See Chapter Three, "Creativity in Love and Freedom."

6. Although some of the following ideas about artistic freedom appear elsewhere in this book, I include them here as well because of their relevance to our discussion of Buñuel and modern art.

Chapter Six

1. Max Klinger, *Graphic Works of Max Klinger* (Magnolia, Mass.: Peter Smith, Plate 72).

Chapter Seven

1. *Op. cit.*, Esslin, *The Theatre of the Absurd,* p. 316.

2. Peter Gay, *The Enlightenment: The Rise of Modern Pragmatism,* I (New York: Knopf, 1966), p. 159.

Chapter Eight

1. See Walter L. Strauss, *The Complete Drawings of Albrecht Dürer,* Volume 4 (1520-1528) (New York: Abaris Books, 1974), pp. 1993-1995.

By the same author:

Art Needs No Justification

In a world of collapsing values all artists agonize over their work. This booklet is a prophetic call to craftsmen, musicians and artists to 'weep, pray, think and work'. 64pp.

Modern Art and the Death of a Culture

In this bestselling book Professor Rookmaaker shows how modern art reflects a whole culture, a dying culture. He builds up a message for our times which may be devastating but is also profoundly positive. He sees above all the tremendous potential and relevance of Christian attitudes, to man, to society, to freedom, to the whole of reality, as the basis for a way ahead in the future. 256pp.